THE STORY

OF THE

THEATRE ROYAL

EXETER

THE STORY

OF THE

THEATRE ROYAL

EXETER

DICK PASSMORE

THE
MINT
PRESS

First published in Great Britain by The Mint Press, 2002

© The Mint Press 2002

The right of Dick Passmore to be identified as author of this
work has been asserted by him in accordance with the Copyright,
Designs & Patents Act 1988.

ISBN 1-903356-21-0

Cataloguing in Publication Data
CIP record for this title is available from the British Library

The Mint Press
18 The Mint
Exeter, Devon
England EX4 3BL

Designed and typeset in New Baskerville 10.5/14
by Mike Dobson, Quince Typesetting

Cover design by Delphine Jones

Printed and bound in Great Britain
by Short Run Press Ltd, Exeter

CONTENTS

DAVID EDMUND

1928–1993

David Edmund was a friend. Not only a friend to those locally who knew him, or worked with him, but also to those many people whom, over many years, he had helped in some little way to gain that extra something from life. In his own quiet, gentle way David passed on his knowledge on so many topics, in the hope that some other person would gain from his wealth of experience.

His many and varied interests ensured that 'spare time' was really non-existent. He could not waste time, spending his hours writing, lecturing, photographing, visiting locations, or generally researching. When he lectured or wrote, the listener or reader could rest assured that David's research would be accurate. If not one hundred per-cent certain of a fact he would either ignore it, or qualify it with an appropriate remark, leaving no doubt as to his uncertainty. Life for him was simply there to be looked into, queried, checked and deliberated.

Born in Leicester, David moved with his family to Exeter in his youth. Largely due to his father, he began a life-long interest in the theatre. This interest was to take him into the professional theatre at the Theatre Royal, Exeter, where he was to become the Chief Electrician and latterly Stage Manager, being employed there until it closed in 1962.

David Edmund was a noted authority on the history of Exeter, and a tutor for the 'Red Coat Guides' of the City Council. He served as chairman of the history section of the Devonshire Association, treasurer of the Devon History Society, and was a founder and former chairman of the Silverton Local History Society. He frequently lectured on many subjects including Exeter's history; the Exeter Blitz, Evacuation, Exeter tramways, local railway, and of course the theatre in Exeter.

For many years he led teams of voluntary back stage workers in local amateur productions and his knowledge of the theatre was demonstrated in his ability to stage shows in the smallest village hall or the most grand theatre. He offered guidance and advice, and had an ability to quietly encourage people to do something with their lives. It would be impossible to number those for whom he made life that little bit easier, but it is ironic that, latterly, life was not made easy for David and he died in 1993.

Friend, colleague or acquaintance – whatever he may have been, David was thought highly of wherever he went. A more gentle, helpful and interesting person would be hard to meet, and he will be long remembered in this city. Some forty years ago a well-loved building passed into oblivion, but its memory lingers even now. For many people, the memory of David Edmund will do likewise.

This book is dedicated to a much-missed friend.

ACKNOWLEDGEMENTS

Such was the popularity of the Theatre Royal that even today, some forty years after it closed, whenever it is mentioned in conversation, or in the local press, anecdotes fly like confetti at a wedding. Many people, knowing of my research, have had interesting snippets to relate, and whilst all of these have been invaluable, they may not necessarily be mentioned here. When so many people have been of assistance it is difficult to prioritise their input, and I make no apology for their names not being listed in any manner of importance. Even if not actually mentioned by name, everyone has my sincere thanks for whatever help they have been able to give.

Jane Iffla, however, has to be mentioned first. I first knew her as a young lady called Jane Crump working backstage at the Theatre Royal, and for many years since she has been a very genuine and kind friend. Jane married David Edmund – the theatre's last stage manager and my introduction to the strange and somewhat unreal world of theatre. Over many years he became a first class friend and mentor. Without Jane and David, this book could never have been published, for much of my research was within the collection and archive that David had built up during his lifetime, and I would have preferred that he had survived to write this story. To be allowed not only to make use of that archive, but also to have it at my home on permanent loan was a bonus. Jane's detailed knowledge of the former theatre was constantly made use of, particularly when checking the draft publication, and I am indebted to her. I am grateful to her husband, John, for his patience!

The amount of time involved in writing such a book is enormous, and Posy, my wife, has endured countless hours of having a husband tucked away in a study writing, researching or on the telephone. During the time that I have been involved in this project, she has also been called upon to look after not only myself during a spell of sickness, but other members of her family, and the past few years have not been easy for her. Nevertheless she has been a constant source of encouragement and help, despite the fact that this has been a labour of love rather than a money-making exercise! She will probably be quite happy never to hear the words *Theatre Royal* again!

Whilst talking families, I must mention my brother, Mike Passmore, who is getting used to a computer illiterate brother being on the end of a telephone! His help in that respect, and his knowledge of the publishing industry has been of great value. Dave Barr has also been constantly called upon, particularly for computer imaging. His technical knowledge and ability has ensured that the countless images and ephemera in the archive will be recorded for posterity.

Many people who either worked at the theatre, or took part in shows there have also had an input, albeit it great or small. Maurice Marshal kindly read the draft and his criticism was, as always, wise and to the point. Harry Hopkins was able to confirm details of the lighting and projection equipment. Several members of the Exeter Amateur Operatic Society have reminded me of certain facts, and for many of them fond memories of the old stage were brought back.

Exmouth resident John Vicary has been a constant source of information and encouragement; Stella Stevenson, from Hemel Hempstead, was probably the first to help me by confirming details of her great grandfather, one of the flymen killed in the theatre fire; Gordon Chapman's intimate knowledge of all things cinematic was called upon in respect of the films shown at the theatre; and I cannot omit the help I have received from staff at the Devon & Exeter Institution, Devon Record Office and the Westcountry Studies Library. These are but a few who have assisted me in some way.

The staff at the Devon & Exeter Institution, Devon Record Office and West-country Studies Library assisted greatly in pointing the way in my research, and Geoff Worrall and Richard Best of the *Express & Echo* have kindly brought the publication to the attention of their readers. The majority of the illustrations have been taken from an archive of Theatre Royal memorabilia that has been privately collected. Whilst every effort has been made to secure permission, it has in a few cases proved impossible to trace the author or the executor. We apologise for any apparent negligence and the publisher invites correspond-ence. Permission to publish images outside of the collection have kindly been given for 4 & 7 by Westcountry Studies Library; 5, Mrs Jane Iffla; 14, Devon Record Office; 15, the Devon Fire and Rescue Service; 19, the Pitts Family; 25, 38, 47, 133, 136, *Express & Echo*; 25, the Stillings Family; 52, *Radio Times*; 112, Mrs Christine Caldwell; 113, Mr and Mrs S. H. Dixon; 123, Peter Thomas by courtesy of the Isca Collection, Exeter. Finally, any book is expensive to produce and I am greatly indebted to the sponsors for providing financial assistance.

PREFACE

In his book *Cavalcade by Candlelight*, E.R. Delderfield concludes with a brief look into what, in 1950, was the future. "Exeter's Theatre", he said, "had a very fine tradition to maintain". At that time the city planners were considering a new Eastgate railway station. If this were to be, then the Theatre Royal site would be needed, which would necessitate the demolition of that building.

Sadly, for other reasons, that was indeed to be the case. The theatre closed in 1962 and was demolished a few months later. Rising within the clouds of dust from the demolition went years of memories, echoes of laughter and nights of sadness. Hard-earned applause passed into oblivion, as did a building beloved by many.

Exeter's seventh theatre, The Northcott, is not in the same "music hall" tradition as the Theatre Royal, and will possibly never be able to enthrall its public in quite the same way as its predecessor did on so many occasions – notably so during the pantomime season. In the same manner, the Theatre Royal buildings in Longbrook Street differed considerably from, and were far superior, to the earlier city theatres.

Delderfield's further statement that "Exeter without its Theatre is as unthinkable as it has been for the last 200 years" is quite interesting. Emphasis should, perhaps, be placed on the word "its" – for Exeter has a theatre still. Yet as we today live in a different era, so we should possibly expect differing standards and presentations; but the Exeter modern theatre-going public has not embraced The Northcott as "its theatre" in the same way as those of previous generations looked upon the Royal.

Times change, and perhaps I, along with countless others, look back with rose-tinted opera glasses; countless others, not merely Exonians, but Devonians and theatre lovers from further a field. We possibly remember only the best of what we witnessed – and why not? We remember the 'stars', the pantomimes and the good times. We no doubt forget the poor audiences, the shows we may not have enjoyed, and the bad times. There was, of course, less in the way of alternative entertainment in the earlier part of the last century. Towards the end of that century, television had started to take its toll, and the public expected more from the entertainment being offered.

Was it right to sell the site and thus close the theatre – or could there possibly have been a reprieve if pressure had been greater? Could more time, or cash, have prevented the closure had either or both been available? Was it something more political than we will ever know? These are questions that have been asked a thousand times without answers. The fact of the theatre's demise cannot be altered by words or thoughts. The lights in that splendid auditorium have dimmed for the last time, the stage has gone – to be set no more. It is strange that havoc created by fire, on no less than three occasions in other city theatres, had been determinedly overcome, yet the demolition by human hand has rendered a final, decisive fate.

The following chapters will give much less detail than other works covering the Exeter's theatres. The deliberate and main intention is to bring back some of the more recent memories, in particular those of the last Theatre Royal – even though Delderfield covered it so well in *Cavalcade by Candlelight*. It is not intended for this to be a detailed historical record of theatre in this city; a potted history, perhaps, but essentially it is a story – the story of Exeter's last 'music hall' theatre. It is a story from which it has been necessary to omit a great deal. Having stood in Exeter for well over seventy years, the Theatre Royal had seen dozens of employees, hundreds of artistes, thousands of shows and countless anecdotes – the majority of which could not possibly be included. The building itself could be the subject of a book, as could the tragic fire or pantomime. Somewhere a line has to be drawn, and it has been necessary to gloss over some aspects readers may well consider essential detail. Almost certainly there will be events, names and facts that some will recall, but that have not been mentioned.

The building was destroyed, but memories, of course, cannot be taken so easily. If, within the ensuing pages, a smile is raised on the reader's face, or a tear brought to the eye, then perhaps the alleged ghost of the Royal will have been re-kindled – on the boards, in the spotlight, and playing again to its audience.

During those years when it stood proud at the top of Longbrook Street, Exeter's Theatre Royal was a special place and brought to many thousands of patrons hours of happiness and enchantment.

Oh no it didn't.........sorry, but oh yes it did!!

R.F.P., 2002

1. *The Theatre Royal, Longbrook Street, at the beginning of the twentieth century. Cab drivers bringing patrons to and from the theatre would rest in the box on the left in New North Road.*

THE EARLY YEARS

William Cotton's *The story of the Drama in Exeter* gives a detailed account of theatre in our city until 1823 – prior to the Longbrook Street days. Eric Delderfield's *Cavalcade by Candlelight* is an excellent history of theatre in Exeter, although Delderfield claims it to be more of a story. He gives great detail of the many artistes who appeared at the various theatres in Exeter, including many of the early stars, and takes the story into the middle of the twentieth century. Both books are essential reading for those who wish to study the history of theatre in Exeter to any great depth. More recently Margaret Toms produced a booklet, entitled *The Seventh Star*, for an exhibition at The Great Hall of Exeter University. This exhibition,

2. Notice of a production of The Beggars Opera *at The Seven Stars, Okehampton Street, Exeter's first "theatre". This is believed to have been the first provincial presentation of Gay's work.*

in 1967, related to the theatres in the City and coincided with the opening of Exeter's seventh theatre, The Northcott. The story can now be brought into the twenty-first century. However, in an attempt to relate the albeit brief 'history' of a comparatively modern theatre, it is necessary to remind the reader of the part played by earlier ones. In true

> BY THE COMPANY OF *Comedians at*
> THE SEVEN STARS, NEAR THE BRIDGE FOOT
> IN ST. THOMAS
> THIS EVENING BEING FRIDAY, NOVEMBER 15TH 1728.
> WILL BE ACTED (FOR THE LAST TIME THIS SEASON.)
> THE BEGGARS OPERA,
> WRITTEN BY INGENIOUS MR. GAY A NATIVE OF DEVON
> WITH ALL THE SONGS AND MUSICK AS PERFORMED-IN THE
> THEATRE ROYAL, LONDON.
> AND BEFORE THE PLAY, AT THE EARNEST REQUEST OF
> DIVERS OF THE GENTRY, MR. RADFORD WILL PERFORM
> HIS AGILITY, WHICH IS THE LAST TIME HE PROPOSES EVER
> TO DO IT IN PUBLICK.
> BEGINNING EXACTLY AT 6 O'CLOCK.
> PRICES 2/S — 1/S — AND SIXPENCE.

pantomime tradition, we have to have a prologue; and as theatres often need the sound of music, let's start at the very beginning!

It is impossible to pinpoint the start of theatre in this city, for various types of performances have been taking place here for many centuries. The registers of Bishop Grandisson in the middle of the fourteenth century show that he was in touch with the Archdeacon on more than one occasion regarding 'malign men' and 'leather-dressers' acting in the city. In 1352 he commanded the Archdeacon to forbid the performance of a 'harmful and blameworthy play... in the Theatre of our City'. Where, or what this 'theatre' was cannot be certain, but it need not have been a building as such, especially as the origin of the word theatre is from the Greek *theatron* – a place for viewing. As in most larger towns and cities throughout the land, Exeter during the sixteenth and seventeenth centuries had its share of strolling players, mummers and visiting companies. Usually these groups performed at public houses, private rooms, in public open spaces or even in the city streets. They would wander from town to town, city to city, presenting their plays, sketches and other acts. In those days it was rare for any town, however large or small, to have a purpose built theatre.

One of the earliest-known Exeter buildings to house a 'theatrical performance' was the Seven Stars public house, then situated in Okehampton Street. It is probable that shows were presented there as early as the turn of the seventeenth and eighteenth centuries. Certainly there is evidence of *The Beggars Opera* being performed there in 1728, and that is thought to have been the

first performance of Gay's masterpiece outside of London. Performances at the Seven Stars took place in an upper room, and on occasions in summer there would be acts in the garden on the banks of the River Exe.

There exists much documentation to show the popularity of this venue, but it is not certain when it ceased to be what can be termed as Exeter's first 'theatre'. The Seven Stars building and other adjacent buildings remained for many more years, until they were eventually purchased by the City Council as part of a road-widening scheme. Although clearance work did start, it

was never finished – at least not by the City council. During those terrible bombing raids on the city by the German Air Force in 1942 that part of Okehampton Street was devastated.

Competition was to be experienced by The Seven Stars in the mid 1700s. Around this time a second theatre appeared, located in the very heart of the city in Waterbeer Street. This street has since gone, but was located at the rear of High Street, running from North Street to Goldsmith Street in what is now the Guildhall Precinct. Little is known of the actual building, although it must have been substantial and almost certainly constructed as a theatre. When the theatre first opened, it was managed by a Mr Kennedy, who is reputed to have also managed theatres in Plymouth and Portsmouth. In 1758 the building was sold to a Mr Pitt, and upon his death was managed by his widow. In 1764, a Mr Jefferson joined her in the management until Mrs Pitt sold her share of the building to a local butcher named Foote. He later purchased Mr Jefferson's share when Jefferson decided to return to London's Drury Lane Theatre. It then passed to a Mr Wolfe and eventually to a Mr Richard Hughes. Hughes was a wealthy gentleman who possessed a keen interest in the theatre.

An early playbill states that the "Exeter Company" was presenting a play entitled *The Wonder* at The Theatre on October 9th 1765. This was some twenty years before the first of the theatres in Bedford Circus opened. It must refer to a building in the Waterbeer Street area for a note at the bottom of the playbill clearly states that 'the way to the Pit is from Goldsmith Street'. The same bill, and similar bills of that period, can be seen to advertise prices of the Boxes (three shillings), Pit (two shillings) and Gallery (one shilling). At one stage in the latter part of its history there was considerable refurbishment of the stage, boxes and pit stalls. There is, then, little doubt that this was a purpose built theatre. The theatre, however, was forced to act somewhat illegally. In 1737 an

Act of Parliament was passed laying down the conditions on where, when and how a place of entertainment could be lawful. Part of this Act concerned any performance put on 'for hire, gain, or reward'. In these circumstances it was required that the building should be licensed. In 1756 a long epistle was produced, addressed to the Citizens of Exeter. This paper went on at great length concerning the 'Lawfulness and Expediency of Frequenting the Theatre in Exeter'.

One or two interesting points arise from it. Firstly, it stated 'that very soon after this Act was passed, the Bath Players, who had been at the Expense of building a Theatre in this City', from which we must assume that the Bath Players were possibly responsible for the Waterbeer Street Theatre. The paper goes on to claim that, in order to avoid patrons paying an admission fee, the Bath Players entered into an agreement with Andrew Brice, a local printer. A keen theatre man, Brice was to produce little packets of what was claimed to be tooth-powder, worm-powder or corn plaster, at prices of 2s., 1/6d., 1/– or 6d. This just happened to be the same prices as the theatre admission charges! Patrons were expected to purchase the tooth powder (or other items) from Brice, and show the wrapper when they entered the 'theatre'. Thus the proprietors were not charging any 'admission fee' to the theatre! What the purchasers did with the contents was their choice, but in the same paper it was also claimed that 'there is no child of ten years in this City...who does not know that Mr Brice's tooth-powder, worm-powder or corn plaster are fit for nothing but to be thrown to the Dung Hill, and are usually disposed of in that manner'!

4. Playbill for the Waterbeer Street theatre, 1765.

The building was not only a theatre, however. John Wesley had visited Exeter on several occasions and his popularity greatly increased the local following of the Methodist movement. Only a few years after the building opened as a theatre, it was taken over by the local Methodists and became a chapel. However, the same Andrew Brice and his followers fought strongly on behalf of the performers. By various means (sometimes fair, but more often a little foul) they were able eventually to regain the building from the Methodists. It was not unknown for hecklers to be in the congregation at some of the Methodists' services, and noisy disturbances often took place outside the chapel, but strangely only when services or meetings were in progress! Eventually the theatre enthusiasts won the day and the building became a theatre once again, and continued as such until 1787. Such was the popularity of the building during that time, that Waterbeer Street had, for a number of years, been known as Theatre Lane. That usage passed when the theatre ceased to exist. There are no visible remains of the theatre as the whole of that side of Waterbeer Street has unfortunately been pulled down, but its location is clearly marked on early maps of the city.

On WEDNESDAY, *October* 9, 1765, at the THEATRE,
Will be presented,
By the EXETER COMPANY,
A COMEDY, call'd

The WONDER:
A Woman keeps a Secret.

Don Felix by Mr. JEFFERSON,
Colonel Briton by Mr. ADCOCK,
Frederick by Mr. ELLARD,
Don Lopez by Mr. HARTRY,
Don Pedro by Mr. FOOT,
Liffardo by Mr. VENABLES,
Gibby by Mr. EDEN,
Vasquez by Mr. EALES,
Alguazile by Mr. CECIL,
Violante by Mrs. BARRY,
Isabella by Miss BAINBRIDGE,
Flora by Mrs. JEFFERSON,
Inis by Mrs. ADCOCK,

End of the Play, a Hornpipe by Miss ADCOC

To which will be added a FARCE call'd

MISS in her TEENS.

Fribble by Mr. JEFFERSON,
Flash by Mr. ELLARD,
Captain Loveit by Mr. ADCOCK,
Puff by Mr. EDEN,
Jasper by Mr. HARTRY,
Miss Biddy Bellair by Miss BAINBRIDGE,
Tag by Mrs. CARTWRIGHT.

The Curtain to be drawn up precisely at Six o'Clock.

BOXES 3s. —— PIT 2s. —— GALLERY 1s.

N. B. TICKETS to be had at Mr. SKINNER's, Jeweller, in the *Fore-ftreet*, at Mrs. HEARD's, Milliner, near *St. John's Bow*; and at the THEATRE, where Places for the Boxes are to be taken (a Book being open'd for that Purpofe) and enter'd, the fame as in *London*, from Ten till Two each Day, by Mr. BARRY.
** The Way to the Pit is from *Goldfmith-ftreet*, from whence alfo, if any Lady Gentleman chooſe it, there is a fmall Paſſage to the Boxes. To the Gallery as ufual.

The Bedford Circus Theatres

The first of what can be regarded as the two 'Bedford Circus' theatres opened in October 1787. They can be regarded as such due to their location.

Prior to the last War, Bedford Circus was one of Exeter's more attractive areas, boasting some fine buildings. A splendid chapel and Georgian town houses had been built in a graceful curve either side of a grassed area, itself enclosed by traditional wrought iron railings. The houses were typical of the Georgian era, with large oblong windows, wrought iron balconies at first floor level and imposing entrances. Towards the Southernhay end of Bedford Circus and on the southern side, was, in much earlier times, the site of the theatres. Following the destruction of the area during the Exeter blitz in 1942, very little of Bedford Circus was left standing. Ghostly facades and empty shells gave way to the inevitable demolition gangs. It was to be re-aligned and re-named Bedford Street. Nothing of the original road remains, and there is nothing to be seen of the original splendour apart from photographs. Now, as a new century breaks, there is talk of yet another demolition gang. Sadly, the plans do not propose a new, elegant Bedford Circus, or even a new theatre, but rather more mundane retail development and housing.

It was in Bedford Circus that the owner of the Waterbeer Street theatre, Richard Hughes, constructed a new theatre. This building was close to the end of Bedford Circus, near its junction with Southernhay, and constructed in brick with a portico supported on six columns. The swept top of the building and hipped roof were in keeping with the period. The former George's Meeting Place, still standing in nearby South Street, is in a similar style, and demonstrates what the theatre must have looked like.

The interior was based on The Sadlers Wells in London. Richard Hughes' father, John Hughes, had been manager at that theatre for some while, and Richard would have known it well. Much of the interior design, therefore, was in a similar vein to that of Sadlers Wells, although it is not known the amount of detail Hughes reproduced in his Exeter building.

5. *The first of the two Bedford Street theatres, damaged by fire in 1820. The buildings on the left are still standing at the junction of Bedford Street and Southernhay West.*

This theatre was somewhat fluctuating in its success. There is no doubt that performances by the likes of Edmund Kean, John and Charles Kemble and their sister, Sarah Siddons played to full houses; yet due to the lack of audiences the theatre was temporarily closed for almost two years towards the end of the eighteenth century. However, it would seem that in the early years of the next century there were signs of improvement, and it continued to thrive for some

6. Fanum House, formerly the headquarters of the Automobile Association, where the two Bedford Circus theatres were located. The pillars shown supporting the façade are similar to those incorporated in the design of the two theatres.

years. Other well-known personalities performed at the theatre in Bedford Circus. One, William Downton, had started his acting career locally, being born in Exeter, but went on to become sought after in several London theatres. Following his long period on the stages of the Metropolis, he became involved in theatre administration in Kent, before returning to the stage. Maria Foote was a very popular actress of the early nineteenth century. She frequently appeared on stages throughout the country, and also made a great impact in London. On many occasions she visited Exeter and performed both here and at other theatres in the South West. A very attractive and elegant lady, she was frequently invited to join wealthy landowners at various events, and eventually married Lord Petersham.

Following the introduction of gas lighting in the city, in 1817 it was decided to install similar lighting in the theatre. Exeter was one of the earliest theatres to do so. Despite the management being eager to adopt modern innovations, it could well have been its undoing. In March 1820, within three years of the introduction of the gas lighting, fire savaged the building. Whilst the exact cause was never discovered, it seems to have been generally accepted at the time that the newly installed gas lighting system was a probability, almost a certainty. The damage was extensive, but the building was under-insured, and insurance did not cover the sum required to rebuild. Despite this, and the amount of damage, sufficient funds were subsequently found to allow the owners to build another theatre on the same site. That was to be the task over the following year.

Thus, in March 1820, fire had claimed its first theatre in Exeter but within a short time another arose from the ashes.

It appears not unusual in this day and age for a building to shoot up seemingly overnight. Modern tech-

7. Playbill for the New Theatre in Bedford Circus, 1789.

For *SIX NIGHTS only*.

FIFTH NIGHT.

NEW THEATRE, Circus, Exeter.

On FRIDAY, *September* the 11th, 1789,

Will be prefented a TRAGEDY, called

The Grecian Daughter

Evander   Mr.   H A G U E,
Philotis   Mr.   D I D D E A R,
Melanthon   Mr.   B E N N E T T,
Phocion   Mr.   F U L L A M,
Arcas   Mr.   J O N E S,
Calippus   Mr.   R   H U G H E S,
And   Dionyfius   Mr.   H O D G K I N S O N,
Erixine   Mifs   H A R R I S O N,

And the Grecian Daughter Mrs. SIDDONS.

To which will be added a FARCE, called

The LYING VALET.

Sharp   Mr.   F U L L A M,
Juftice Guttle   Mr.   H A G U E,
Beau   Trippet   Mr.   D I D D E A R,
Drunken Cook Mr. R. H U G H E S,
And   Gaylefs   Mr.   B E N N E T T,
Melifa   Mifs   K E Y S,
Mrs.   Gadabout   Mrs.   H U G H E S,
Mrs.   Trippet   Mifs   S.   K E Y S,
And   Kitty   Pry   Mifs   H A R R I S O N.

The DOORS to be opened at SIX o'Clock, and the Curtain drawn up precifely at SEVEN.

BOXES 3s.—PIT 2s.—GALLERY 1s. 6d.

. No Places can be book'd without Tickets being taken for the refpective Night at the Time.

☞ TICKETS for each Night to be had of Mr. TREWMAN, Printer and Bookfeller, and of Mr. Jones Kemp, Box-Keeper, of whom Places may be taken at the Theatre every Day from Twelve a One, and at any other Part of the Day at his Houfe in the Gayfter.

†‡† Nothing under FULL PRICE will be taken during the whole Performance.

No BOX TICKET to be admitted to any other Part of the Houfe.

EXETER: Printed by A. TREWMAN and SON.

niques, equipment and ability make such happenings almost essential for cost-effectiveness. It would seem quite incredible, however, to read that within twelve months of the first Bedford Circus theatre being destroyed, the second was finished and ready to take in patrons. It should be borne in mind that this was well over one hundred and seventy years ago, when although labour was comparatively cheap, there were no technological aids to the building trade as there are today. Horses and carts transported materials, which were

8. Sarah Siddons, the well-known actress who appeared at Exeter in the late eighteenth century.

taken around a building site by hand, not machinery. There were no concrete mixers, no mechanical diggers, and no easy way to do anything, just sheer hard work and long hours.

The new building was a much more elaborate affair, with arches and columns supporting an ornate frontage. Arched recesses over the front of the building housed statues. The portico columns are thought to have been salvaged from the original building. Here should be mentioned an interesting fact. The Bedford Circus theatres were on the same location as the building in today's Bedford Street known as Fanum House and formerly the local headquarters of the Automobile Association, now a sports clothing shop. Curiously, this modern building does in fact have columns at the front supporting the upper storeys. There are few modern buildings in Exeter where external columns are used as supports, but as this was the location of the 'Bedford Circus' theatres, could it be that the architect was aware of the old theatre façades when he was designing the modern building? It may have been pure coincidence of course, but even if that is the case, it nevertheless adds to the interest of Exeter theatres!

In January 1821 the new theatre opened – to be known first as the *New Theatre, The Circus,* but later to become Exeter's first *Theatre Royal.* Within a comparatively short time it too suffered dwindling audiences, and in 1823, in similar circumstances to that of its predecessor, it was forced to close for a short while.

It appears once again that, as with the former theatre, when the building was re-opened the audiences improved and the management of a Mr Brunton successfully steered the theatre towards profit. Well-known actors and actresses took their place on the stage, and in particular two gentlemen, one by the name of William Macready and the other the aforementioned Edmund Kean, were regular visitors. Kean had by this time become a fine serious actor, although a somewhat sad character in real life. Temperamental and moody, and a little too fond of imbibing, he was nevertheless a national figure, appearing in many theatres throughout the country. His portrayal of Shylock was, at that time,

9. Edmund Kean, noted actor of the early nineteenth century, who attracted large audiences in Exeter.

said to be the best ever seen in English Theatre.

The theatre was forced to change in order to keep its audiences. Despite the gallant attempts of theatre managers to encourage patrons, times were different and often difficult. The public sensed change wherever they went, and were increasingly aware of what they wanted. It was amidst this unsettled background that disaster was to strike yet again.

During a time when theatre was not a booming success, and finances were often strained, fire once more devastated Exeter's Theatre. As on the previous occasion there were, thankfully, no personal injuries – although it is said that the show at the time, *Beauty and the Beast*, included a pig that died during the blaze. Here again, there is no actual evidence as to the cause of the fire, but the building was reduced to just the four external walls. Once again, the insurance cover on the building could not cover the cost of rebuilding. Eventually it was to become a drill hall, until destruction during the wartime blitz in 1942, when much of Bedford Circus disappeared. Thus it was that, in February 1885, Exeter's theatre-going public was again to be denied their theatre.

Yet, once more, we have to admire the speed and efficiency with which a new building was to be constructed. For, according to the records, it was just over twelve months from the destruction of the second Bedford Circus building that Exeter witnessed the creation of another Exeter theatre. This new building was to be in a different location, and of an entirely different design and construction. Larger, purpose built and with the backing of a newly appointed company, it was nevertheless to have a similar history to its predecessors – although few would have believed that possible at the time.

10. An artist's impression of the second theatre in Bedford Circus. Like its predecessor, it was also the victim of fire.

THE FIRST LONGBROOK STREET THEATRE

Despite the fluctuations of audiences and the ensuing financial problems, there seemed no cessation of interest in recreating theatres! Late in 1885, following the fire in the second Bedford Circus theatre, a company was formed – the *Exeter Theatre Company* – that was to remain in control of Exeter's main theatre for almost eighty years. The company was able to raise finance to purchase a site on which they would have constructed a grand new theatre, the second Theatre Royal and the fifth theatre in the city.

The Exeter Theatre Company announced that their chosen site had already been acquired at the junction of New North Road and Longbrook Street and it was here that they proposed the new theatre would stand. They engaged the services of one of most prominent theatre architects in the country, Charles J. Phipps Esq., FSA. The site was quite large, and the architect persuaded the directors that it would be beneficial to let part of the ground as it would not be required, and could generate additional income. This was to prove unwise, as that space could have provided additional backstage accommodation for paint rooms, carpentry workshops and storage, away from the main theatre building. It would also have made more space available for better facilities in the remaining parts of the Theatre. Added to that, the rental received was a mere £35 per annum.

The building was soon constructed and although it was to stand on that site for a considerable number of years, it was to have an even more chequered history than any of its predecessors. After just twelve short months, the structure

11. Architect's drawing of the exterior of the first Theatre Royal in Longbrook Street which was ravaged by fire in September 1887.

12. Interior auditorium plan of the theatre, 1886. The dress circle was far more horseshoe shaped than the second theatre. The gallery seats can be seen at the rear of the dress circle.

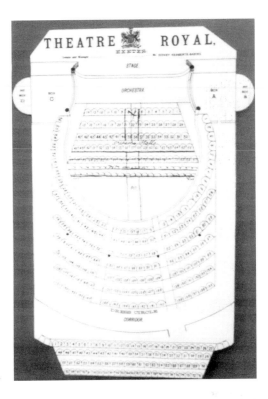

was to change dramatically, the changes not being at the mere whim of the company directors, but the result of something far more serious, as will be seen.

The foundation stone was laid in May 1886, and in October there was great excitement as the new theatre was opened. It had cost a reputed £7,300 to build, although the original estimate of the architect had been £6,500. The building work had been entrusted to a Mr Bevan of Plymouth. The auditorium (which was able to seat around fifteen hundred people) and the stage were both much larger than those of the previous theatres. They were designed and constructed in the hope of enticing larger productions to the West, which in turn were expected to attract larger audiences. Larger audiences meant more profit. The building was the largest theatre Exeter had known, allegedly constructed to the best design possible at that time.

Far more grand and imposing than the previous theatres in Bedford Circus, it occupied a position in the centre of a busy and thriving city. Artists' impressions of the building suggest that whilst the outside was not spectacular, the interior was typical of the large London theatres, many still in use today. The architect had contrived to give the impression of the Italian renaissance. A huge central domed ceiling was covered in attractive plaster carvings of foliage and other decorative designs. Private boxes had heavy velvet, swagged curtains that blended well with the gold and cream finishing of the plasterwork around them. The balconies were swept around the theatre in the traditional almost semi-circular shape, and the walls had large areas of carved plasterwork. Massive amounts of ornately carved plaster mouldings, panels and coving adorned much of the auditorium, whilst those areas of the walls not so adorned are said to have been covered with a deep crimson wallpaper that resembled linen. The proscenium arch and side panels were again decorated in gold and cream,

13. Architect's longitudinal plan of the theatre, 1885.

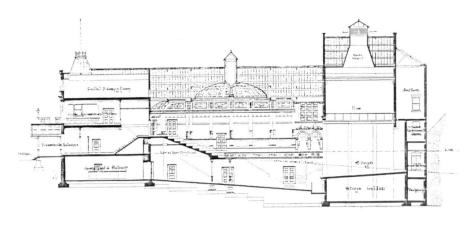

with fluted columns and much floral plaster carving. Much of the seating had been upholstered by local craftsmen, and matched the red velvet of the curtains in the private boxes. When Mayor Richard Daw opened the theatre, the completed interior must have been something to behold – truly rich in style, colour and design. It was in complete contrast to Exeter's previous theatres.

It was during this latter part of the nineteenth century that theatrical touring companies came into their own. These companies came mainly from London and the bigger cities, theatres in the provinces using them more and more to entice larger audiences. They would tour, often for several weeks, presenting varied programmes to audiences far and wide.

The Theatre Royal in Longbrook Street had been operating for almost a year when a touring company opened there in what was to become, locally, a famous production. It was famous, however, for the wrong reasons. The latter months of 1887 were to become a nightmare for many people. Those dark months of sadness and grief were to go down in the annals of English theatre history. In that short period of time, Exeter was to attract the attention of the government, the national and international press, and the general public in a manner which has probably only been equalled by the havoc created as a result of Hitler's revenge in 1942. For, almost unbelievably, fire was to be responsible for the destruction of yet another theatre in the City. On this occasion, however, it was not just a building that was lost. Lost, too, were the lives of many of Exeter's citizens.

The Theatre Fire

Unlike theatre today, it was customary in the nineteenth century for an "evening" performance to mean just that. Theatres would sometimes open as early as six o'clock, and performances could continue late into the evening, perhaps until midnight. Patrons certainly got their money's worth, and it was common for more than one show to be performed in an evening. On the 5th September 1887, however, there was only one show to see. Mr Gilbert Elliott had brought his company to Exeter to perform the popular drama *Romany Rye*. It opened that evening to a virtually full house. What followed has become a very well documented and renowned part of Exeter's theatrical history. For several agonizing weeks it was also headline news throughout the country, and it must have seemed as if the eyes of the country were focused on this city for the remainder of that year.

Towards the end of that evening's performance, allegedly sometime close to 10.30, (depending on which

14. *Detail from the programme for* Romany Rye, *the show being presented by Mr Gilbert Elliott's Company at the time of the fire in 1887.*

10

*15. Local artist Fred Ford
created this splendid image
of the theatre fire in 1887.
It was reproduced by the
Devon Fire and Rescue
Service as a limited edition
print in 1987.*

report is accurate), part of the set was being changed. As is customary, one of
the cast – in this case a character called *Scragger* – was down-stage of a cloth,
acting out the scene change. This is simply a brief scene in front of a cloth,
routinely included within any show in order to give the back-stage team enough
time to change the set.

At this point in the show there were loud noises from behind the front
cloth, but there were occasions backstage when, unintentionally, parts of a
scene dropped or fell whilst the scene was being set. Naturally the audience
thought it quite amusing, as was often the case. They were even more amused
when a backcloth fell from behind the top of the proscenium arch on to the
stage, narrowly missing *Scragger*. Their amusement, however, was soon turned
to concern when the cloth, in front of which *Scragger* was acting his part, billowed
out towards the auditorium. It was at that point that some of the audience was

*16. A wood engraving
from* The Illustrated
London News.

17. Exterior view on the morning after the fire. Charred brickwork around window openings is clearly visible.

able to see fire on stage. At first it was visible to only a few. But of course those few who did see it were readily aware of what was happening and quickly told others what they had seen. Within seconds shouts of 'fire' were coming from patrons in the auditorium, and people started to leave the theatre. Their concern quickly grew to panic, and in a very short space of time the whole audience realized that the stage was alight.

The audience tried to leave at the same time, but the fire spread so quickly that within no time at all it reached the auditorium. Much of the internal construction was dry, flammable material, feeding the hungry flames. The various reports show that whilst the majority of patrons were lucky in being able to escape quickly, many others were less fortunate. Some, who made good their exit from the fire, lost their lives trying to assist others. Those in the gallery had a particular problem as any exit there was limited, and on the Longbrook Street side there were no exits at all. The one flight of stairs from the gallery had three turns, twisting virtually back on itself, and some way down was partially blocked by a pay box and a post – said to have been installed after the final inspection by licensing magistrates. It is said that this pay box was portable and the crowd had actually knocked it over, causing even more

IN TENDER AND LOVING REMEMBRANCE
OF THOSE
Men, Women, and Children,
Who perished in the dreadful Conflagration in the
EXETER THEATRE,
On Monday Night, September 5, 1887.

" In the midst of life we are in death."

18. In true Victorian tradition, these cards were distributed following the fire in memory of those who lost their lives.

problems. The design itself restricted the width of the staircase, allowing only one or two abreast at any given time, making their exit at normal speed. On this occasion it was not just one or two; it was a mass of many dozen patrons in sheer panic, each trying to get out as fast as possible, probably with total disregard for anyone else. Had there been a second exit from the gallery, there is little doubt that more lives would have been saved.

Some patrons were lucky enough to scramble on to a balcony at the front of the building, from where they were rescued by ladder. Elsewhere, others jumped from windows to escape; some tried to jump from the roof; and many were trampled underfoot in the rush to reach exits. Little doubt this was hysteria in its worst form. Many are believed to have gone through various doors that led to other parts of the building, thinking they were exits. For those poor souls there was of course no return. They were trapped in the inferno. Some exit doors opened inwards, thus hampering attempts to open them as dozens of patrons pressed towards those exits, trying to escape into the fresh air they knew to be not far away.

19. Fire tender known as "Little West", 1807. Owned by the Pitts family who operated the former Trews Weir paper mills, Exeter. This machine was last used at the theatre in 1887 and is now displayed at the Norwich Union Insurance Company building in Barnfield Road.

It was not until the following day that the entirety of the dreadful carnage emerged. It was painfully obvious that as the building contained so much timber, very little remained of the interior. The gaunt shell was virtually the only part that remained intact, a stark reminder of that night's tragedy.

Some 180 bodies were found, but there can be little doubt that many more had perished without trace, such was the intensity of the fire. It has been claimed that only a third of the bodies recovered could actually be recognized and identified. *The Western Daily Mercury* issued a special edition the following day. It reported that the task of searching the ruins continued through the night, but in some cases mere fragments were recovered, the actual bodies having been almost wholly consumed and totally impossible to identify. The majority of the cast appeared to have escaped with little injury, although Mr Gilbert Elliott himself was badly burned. The newspaper also claims that it was likely that of the 190 believed to be in the gallery, probably 140 perished. That would seem to be quite reasonable, for it was the exits from the gallery that caused so many problems. Those in the pit and stalls would have had far more chance to escape into Longbrook Street and New North Road, as did Mr Monilot, the actor playing *Scragger*.

During the following week, the story was told in detail by the various local newspapers. Additionally, *The Illustrated London News*, *The Graphic*, *The Pall Mall Gazette* and *The Penny Illustrated Paper* were just four of the many national journals that also gave considerable coverage to the fire. It was compared with the Paris Opera fire of that year, the fire at the Ring Theatre, Vienna, in 1881, and another at the Moscow Theatre. In these, and other theatre fires over a period of some eleven years, over two thousand people perished. The journals also carried a number of artistic impressions of the Exeter building burning, and

20. Artist's impression of the gutted stage, viewed from the dress circle.

the aftermath. Artists went sent to Exeter by the national newspapers including Messrs Jones and Brown from *The Graphic*, Mr Melton Prior of *The Illustrated London News* and Mr George Thompson of *The Pall Mall Gazette*.

At the time of the fire, heroic attempts to save lives were made; two such heroes were William Hunt and Bombardier Scattergood, the latter having perished in the disaster. Another was Driver George Cooper, also of the Royal Artillery, the regiment then stationed at Higher Barracks – just a short distance from the Theatre.

Time and again these people, and many others, returned to the inferno and helped save lives, although sadly not all the rescue attempts were successful. Their actions, and the actions of many others at the scene, have been well documented. No one would doubt the courage of such heroic acts in those grim surroundings. Firemen also played a large part in the rescue operation. It seems rather basic and primitive to us now that those brigades attending the fire came from all over the City, and even as far as Topsham. Horses, clattering through the dark City streets in their haste to assist, hauled some of the appliances. Others were literally manhandled, pulled by those courageous men who were to assist in attempts to quell the blaze. It is said that men of the

21. Interior showing the front cloth bellowing out at the start of the fire, when flames could be seen on stage by the audience.

Topsham brigade started to pull their appliance by hand, as the horses had to be brought from a field and harnessed before they were able to join the men on the road towards Exeter! It is difficult to picture these scenes, and even more so to imagine hauling the appliances up even the slightest incline, or even worse trying to control one downhill. It is through no fault of those firemen that by the time they had reached the Theatre, the whole building was well ablaze, and no matter how gallant their efforts, there was no way that it could have been prevented.

Whilst much has been written concerning the 'heroes' of that night, few words have been recorded about those backstage workers who also attempted – albeit in vain – to stop the fire spreading. Little is actually known about this aspect of the tragedy, apart from those details that emerged at the Coroner's Inquest – and even that is scant.

According to records available, the fire started when some drapes, or part of a cloth, came into direct contact with the 'fish tail' gas burners that helped light the stage. These burners were open gas flames, protected only by a basic cage over the front, and were commonplace in theatres and other buildings of that era. Two flymen, those backstage workers high up over the stage in what is known as the flies, taking scenery in and out on ropes, appear to have noticed the fire first. John Taylor and Thomas Warren were unable to attract the attention of other backstage personnel, and were hampered in their attempts to quell the outbreak by the lack of equipment available for extinguishing fires. (It transpired at the Inquest that the backstage area was not the only part of the theatre the architect left sadly lacking in such equipment.) In their attempts to prevent the fire spreading, Taylor and Warren cut loose the ropes of a nearby cloth that then fell onto the stage. It was that cloth which had been seen falling by the audience during *Scragger's* performance.

Despite their brave attempts to quell the fire, both flymen perished in the ensuing inferno. A third flyman, Wesley Bates, somehow survived and gave evidence at the Coroner's Inquest. Taylor and Warren undoubtedly did their best to warn of the fire having started, and tried their utmost to prevent it spreading. Taylor, who lived in Frog Street, left a widow and six young children. Warren left a widow and two children.

On that fateful evening, John Taylor, Thomas Warren and many others on stage did whatever they were able to suppress the fire. Elsewhere, others made brave attempts to rescue those trapped inside. In many cases, instinctive and unselfish reactions resulted in the loss of many innocent lives. It would have been easy for Taylor and Warren to flee once they saw the beginnings of the fire; Hunt, Scattergood and Cooper could have merely walked away. They all chose not to, putting themselves in total danger. At a special meeting of the city council in Guildhall the day after the fire, Mr Russell Rosse, a member of Mr Gilbert Elliott's company, said:

> I wish to say at this point that the two men who worked 'the flies' at the Theatre, and who were the first on apprehending the danger to lower the curtain, have, I am sorry to say, lost their lives. They had the presence of mind to lower the curtain to prevent the people seeing the flames, and after that the two men disappeared behind the flies and were never seen again afterwards.

Their bravery, and of the many others who attempted to save those trapped inside and on top of the building, will long be remembered. Some were fortunate enough to survive, but many lost their lives trying to save others. Immediately after the fire, and during the Inquest, several survivors recalled the sad events of that evening. However, one of the more fortunate patrons that night gave his version of the fire much later. Mr A.W. Jarrett was, at the time, a reporter for *The Western Morning News* and later to become Editor of the *Devon & Somerset News*. In 1935, aged 72, he recalled his involvement in the tragedy quite vividly:

Calamitous Fire

AT THE

THEATRE ROYAL, EXETER

On the 5th SEPTEMBER 1887.

PRUDENTIAL ASSURANCE COMPANY LIMITED

HOLBORN BARS, LONDON.

INVESTED ASSETS EXCEED ...   ...   £7,000,000.
CLAIMS PAID EXCEED   ...   .   £9,000,000.

Total number of Lives lost 140, of whom 55 were Assured in this Company.

LIST OF CLAIMS.

Name of Deceased.	Address.	£	s.	d.
Baker, John R.	93 Summerland Street ... ...Exeter	9	18	0
Bale, Henry J.	Coombe Street ... ... „	8	11	0
Berry, Louisa	Pancras Lane ... ... „	10	14	0
Bennillick, James	Tabernacle Court, Coombe Street ... „ ...	7	12	0
Bennillick, Matilda	„ „ ... „ ...	9	2	0
Bennillick, George H.	„ „ ... „ ...	9	6	0
Blatchley, Harriet	Preston Street ... ... „	11	2	0
Blatchley, Edward	„ ... ... „	14	6	0
Chapple, John C.	10 Rack Street ... ... „	10	7	0
Cork, James...	Shillhag, Commercial Road ... ... „ ...	10	0	0
Dart, Harriet	44 Coombe Street ... ... „	7	3	0
Dart, Joseph E.	„ ... ... „	6	10	0
Davie, Sarah	7 Oakfield Street, Heavitree ... „ ...	6	14	0
Davie, Harry P.	„ ... ... „ ...	11	16	0
Davie, William H.	„ ... ... „ ...	2	10	0
Edworthy, Mary A.	Prospect Place, Rack Street ... ... „	7	11	0
Elston, John D.	South Wonford, Heavitree ... ... „	7	12	0
Elston, Rhoda	„ „ ... ... „	10	8	0
Evans, James H.	9 Paul Street ... ... „	15	12	0
Froom, James	Chudley's Court, Coombe Street ... „	13	18	0
Hannaford, Ann	Exe Island ... ... „	18	12	0
Hannaford, George	„ ... ... „	15	18	0
Harris, Alfred	4 Hampton Place, North Street ...Exeter	10	5	0
Havill, Sarah	52 Preston Street ... ... „ ...	7	16	0
Hickman, William R.	8 North Bridge, Saint David's Hill ... „	15	4	0
Hickman, Rosa	„ „ ... „	18	4	0
Lake, John	33 Preston Street ... ... „ ...	13	12	0
Lake, Charles H. T.	33 „ ... ... „ ...	2	10	0
Lashbrook, John	3 Chudley's Court, Coombe Street ... „	6	10	0
Lee, Christiana	34 Coombe Street ... ... „ ...	1	8	0
Ley, Margaret	Day's Court, Frog Street ... ... „	2	16	0
Ley, Edward J.	Frog Street ... ... „ ...	6	0	0
Lipscombe, Mary J.	Melbourne Street ... ... „ ...	10	5	0
Lockyer, Mark	3 Mary Arches Street ... ... „ ...	10	14	0
Lyons, Edward	Ewing's Lane ... ... „ ...	11	10	0
Miller, Amelia	Gibbs Court, Paris Street ... ... „	8	1	0
Millman, Joseph	52 Coombe Street ... ... „ ...	7	16	0
Mortimore, Elizabeth	2 Chudley's Court ... ... „ ...	3	14	0
Parsons, James S.	Coffins Court, Smythen Street ... „	13	6	0
Pepperill, Harriet...	Barbican Court, Paul Street ... ... „	10	13	0
Phillips, Enos	36 Coombe Street ... ... „ ...	9	10	0
Pollard, William G.	Church Hall, Rack Street... ... ... „	9	16	0
Rawlins, John T.	West Street ... ... „ ...	10	8	0
Rawlins, Sarah	„ ... ... „ ...	9	14	0
Rice, Walter	Bartholomew Street ... ... „ ...	11	2	0
Rice, Charles	West Gate ... ... „ ...	4	0	0
Stephens, Frederick H.	1 Clarence Place, Well Lane ... ... „	11	2	0
Taylor, John Fred.	Frog Street ... ... „ ...	51	17	0
Taverner, Thomas H.	Penitentiary Court, Holloway Street ... „	10	10	0
Tout, Edwin T.	39 Mary Arches Street ... ... „ ...	9	6	0
Tucker, William J.	15 Goldsmith Street ... ... „ ...	10	5	0
Tucker, Thomas	37 Preston Street ... ... „ ...	8	14	0
Warren, Thomas	Paul's Place, Paul Street ... ... „ ...	11	10	0
Wood, John J.	Plantation Buildings, New Town ... ... „	1	10	0
Wood, William H.	„ „ ... „	7	12	0
		£ 562	2	0

W. C. & Co.—40, 9-87.

22. *List of claims by families of fire victims made against the Prudential Assurance Company Ltd., which was to eventually purchase the theatre site for development.*

I occupied a front seat in the stalls. Between the second and fourth acts I left the Theatre, and soon after I had returned I saw the drop scene fall almost on Mr Graham's head as he was speaking his lines. He finished what he had to say after the curtain had passed his face, and I remarked to a friend 'What a strange thing! I never saw that occur before.' At the same moment the curtain came forward with a great 'puff' and seemed to graze my forehead. I saw at the sides sparks and flame, and heard a crackling noise.

Realising at once the terrible nature of the incident, I rushed for the door and was over the stairs in a moment. When I reached the passage on a level with the dress circle I saw there was a frightful rush for the front exit and I turned into a passage on the right which I knew led to the special escape doors in New North Road. I fell while going over the stairs and reached the street exhausted. Just as I reached the big doors they were thrown back, but by whom I cannot say. The scene in the doorways and on the outside balconies, which were crowded with men and women – mostly women piteously calling for help, and with the flames near enough to burn and scorch them – was simply heartrending.

The proprietor of the near-by New London Inn, Mr Robert Pople, was praised for his part in assisting the firefighters and rescuers. He readily gave over the whole of the courtyard and stable block of his premises to assist those responsible for laying out the dead and caring for the injured. The New London Inn was a substantial and fine building that has long since vanished, as has London Inn Square, where it once stood. That night, the elegant surroundings of one of Exeter's most prestigious hotels must have taken on a sombre and eerie mantle.

Although most of the reports and stories in the press concerning the fire were, by their very substance, grim and forbidding, there was one report that would have been almost hilarious had it not been for the surrounding circumstances. On Tuesday, September 13th 1887, the Reverend John Ingle, the Rector of St Olaves church (and one time principal of Mount Radford School in St Leonards), appeared before Justices at The Castle. The charge brought against him was that 'on September 8th he was drunk in Exeter Cemetery on the occasion of the burial of several victims of the Exeter Theatre fire'.

In evidence for the prosecution, the Rural Dean, Revd Mallett, stated that he first saw Ingle walking at the head of a funeral party with "a staggering gait", and "mumbling" words. Mallett, himself conducting a funeral service, was later approached by mourners who complained that Ingle was acting very strangely, smelt of alcohol and seemed barely able to read the burial service. After three attempts, he is alleged to have given up and walked unsteadily away! The report claims that several mourners shouted after him to come back and finish the service, whilst others were so disgusted that they wanted him thrown into the grave with the coffin! The Rural Dean took Ingle to the cemetery chapel, where they awaited the arrival of police officers. Ingle was then removed from the cemetery by the officers, and sent home by cab.

At the hearing, Reverend Ingle conducted his own defence and totally denied being intoxicated. His wife gave evidence to the effect that at lunch on that day (the burials being mid-afternoon) her husband "had consumed but one glass of beer and a glass and a half of port wine". Others confirmed that he was very much sober. Ingle told the Justices that he had been mentally and physically ill for some twelve months, and on the two nights previous to the incident he had not slept. In addition, he claimed the "ghastly sight of rows of coffins in the cemetery had positively unnerved him". The Justices retired for a while, and then announced that in their opinions the evidence was conflicting, and that any doubt should go in favour of the defendant. They dismissed the case, to applause from the public gallery!

The Fire Report

> "Oh, Captain Shaw! Type of true love kept under, could thy brigade,
> with cold cascade, quench my great love, I wonder…"

So sings the Queen of the Fairies in *Iolanthe*. The Captain Shaw referred to in that song was an actual person, held in high esteem by the London society of that era. Captain Eyre Massey Shaw, C.B., was the Chief Officer of the Metropolitan Fire Brigade in London. He had been staying in Exeter on the night of the disaster, and was instructed by the Secretary of State for the Home Department (now the Home Office), to enquire into the fire, and submit a full report to the Government.

His subsequent report was dated 29th September 1887, a mere 24 days after the incident. The report covers nineteen foolscap sheets, and in all probably over 15,000 words. At that time there were no electronic innovations to assist him. There were no tape recorders, no computers, and photography was still in its infancy. It was a formidable task. To attend the scene, make what was obviously a painstaking and in-depth enquiry, confirm the multitude of points arising from that enquiry, and report back within three weeks must have been a massive exercise.

Captain Shaw's report goes into great detail and seemingly leaves no stone unturned. He showed no tendency to gloss over anything that he considered a contributory factor, and made no attempt to hide any point he considers valid, and names anyone, or anything, he feels at fault. After the preamble, Shaw reports on the findings of the Coroner's Jury and then presents his own report. (The Inquest itself is subject of a later chapter.)

In the first few paragraphs, Captain Shaw explained why his job was more difficult than usual. Firstly, the theatre had been virtually destroyed. Secondly, the drawings and plans had not been totally adhered to, and as there had been 'many alterations and additions in almost all parts of the theatre', it was necessary to carry out much research within the ruins. Thirdly, he had received no specification or information detailing the works and materials used, making it virtually impossible for him to ascertain if they were of the required standard.

The local Licensing Authority had ordered the building to be constructed in accordance with the rules and regulations of the Metropolitan Board of Works. There were seventeen regulations, the majority of which concerned safety aspects. The architect claimed that these 'only applied to buildings constructed in London'. However, Captain Shaw pointed out that as the Authority had ordered the theatre to be built in accordance with them,

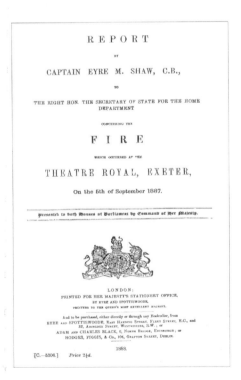

23. Cover of Fire Report prepared for the government by Captain Eyre M. Shaw, CB.

this was part of the architect's contract, and should have been complied with by Mr Phipps.

When the Licensing Authority visited the building, the alterations were alleged by the architect to have been made before the licence was granted, although there can be little reason to believe that this was so. Some of the alterations would have had a direct bearing on the fire. In brief, some of the requirements were:

    a. That an additional exit was needed from the area of the pit stalls, orchestra stalls and private boxes;

    b. Exits into Longbrook Street were required to be at least 6 feet wide;

    c. Two doorways in the dress circle should have been altered so that each consisted of two doors, not one (thus taking up less space when opened);

    d. The two fire hydrants in the theatre should have hose pipes of eighty feet, not forty;

    e. An additional exit should be provided from the gallery, by converting an existing window into a door.

The theatre was not totally finished when opened to the public, and it was several months before the architect issued his completion certificate to the builder. Even then, there is no doubt that the certificate was of little worth, as the approved plans were not adhered to, and thus the building was not in compliance with the original planning consent.

Captain Shaw states that the inclusion of six shops on the ground floor in the Longbrook Street frontage was a mistake. This could have provided an area for more exits from the auditorium. 'The shops', said Capt. Shaw, 'contributed in no small degree to this sad calamity'. Even for those with no knowledge of building it is plain to see from the plans that exits on the Longbrook Street side were sadly lacking. Let us take a little time looking at just a few of the other faults Captain Shaw found – and this is by no means a comprehensive list.

A ventilator shaft in the roof of the theatre had not been fitted with suitable cowls to prevent down draughts. Had this been done, and the whole roof built a few feet higher than it was, it would have assisted the smoke to ascend and escape out of the building rather than spread to other parts of the auditorium. The wall of the proscenium arch should have been a minimum of thirteen inches throughout, but in places was only nine. There was apparently only one metal clad door in the whole building – and that was not strengthened, so buckled easily in the intense heat. Had the Regulations been followed, several staircases would have been constructed in fireproof materials, yet were in fact wooden. Two doorways, under the stage in the proscenium arch wall were not on the plans. These openings had wooden doors that, having been burnt, would have allowed flames to shoot out into the auditorium area instead of being retained behind the wall. The scene dock (a storage area for scenery) at the rear of the stage area was not separated from the main stage in any way. The regulations required a brick and fire-proof separation. Above the stage in the flies, there were no fire hydrants or other means of extinguishing any fire. On the architect's plans a fire hydrant was shown to be on the side of the flies, but none had ever been fixed there. To one side at the rear of the stage were two carpenter's benches, and another space used as a paint shop. It was estimated by an employee that about half a ton of wood shavings, loose wood and debris was on the floor that evening (although half a ton of such material seems a slight exaggeration). Some corridors were 3'6" wide, the walls of which were, in places, of lath and plaster, and in other places matchwood. The Regulations stated all corridors should be of fireproof construction and a minimum 4'6" in width. The gallery should have had a staircase either side, but there was only one, and that was obstructed in several places.

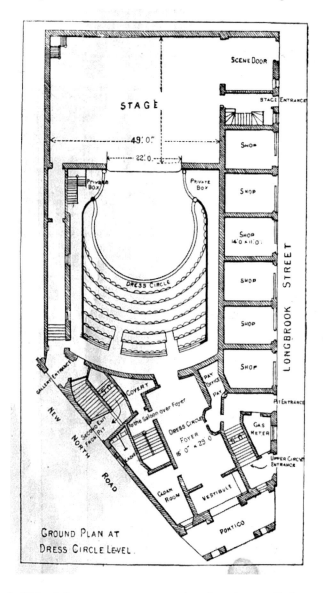

24. Architect's plan of the first theatre in Longbrook Street. Integral shops are shown on the Longbrook Street side and were an important factor in the fire of 1887. Capt. Shaw's report into the fire criticised their inclusion as it prevented any exits from that side of the building.

Paragraph 236 of the report sums up the situation well. It states "the fire arose in the flies through accident or neglect on the part of those employed [the architect and builders, and not those employees backstage that evening] and the heavy loss of life was caused by the bad construction of the theatre".

Captain Shaw, in his conclusion, listed twelve factors instrumental in either the cause of the fire, or in assisting its spread. He also stated that "…in his experience of fire fighting, any one of these serious defects of construction should have prevented the licensing of the building as a theatre". He continued "it may be, as stated in the evidence, that there are elsewhere other theatres as bad as that of Exeter; but it may be confidently asserted that there can be very few worse." That itself was quite a damning statement.

The report does not specifically name any licensing magistrate, but local press reports suggest that those who actually granted the licence were Messrs. Lang, Knapman, Westron, Peters and Thomas. However, it appears (from evidence at the Inquest) that various magistrates had been involved in visiting the Theatre prior to granting the licence, their purpose being "to ensure the building was fit for the purpose intended". It would appear also that, as the magistrates had no professional advice in ensuring that the building was safe – and indeed the law did not require them to have such advice, it rested merely on their visual inspection. Despite their requirement that some alterations be made, the licence was nevertheless issued on the promise of that being done, but of course it transpired that such alterations never were carried out.

Although Captain Shaw was quite openly and seriously concerned by the defects of construction (and the part played by Phipps, the architect, in such defects), he did tend finally to lay the blame firmly on the shoulders of the Licensing Authority. By their granting of a licence to the Exeter Theatre Company, it was presumed that they considered the building safe for public performances. Captain Shaw considered that they either deceived themselves, or were deceived, and that "even with the most ordinary care they ought to have discovered that, according to the rules which they themselves had adopted, the building was unfit to be licensed as a theatre".

In any event, Captain Shaw undoubtedly considers that the ultimate responsibility is with the Authority, and paragraph 244 of the report is worthy to quote:

> Notwithstanding the verdict of the Jury, it must again be stated plainly that on a certain date the licensing authority assumed the whole and sole responsibility for the safety of life in the Exeter Theatre, and by that act relieved the [Exeter Theatre] Company and all those who were employed by the Company, including the architect and all others whom I have mentioned.

That paragraph on its own is no more than a précis of the findings in Captain Shaw's most detailed and interesting report. It seems to plant the blame for the fire firmly on the shoulders of the Licensing Magistrates.

It was as a result of Captain Shaw's report into the fire, and the serious design errors found, that the Home Department in London felt obliged to draft new regulations for theatres. Many still exist today – exit signs shall be illuminated, doors shall open outwards, safety curtains should be installed and so on. There is a slight question regarding the introduction of safety curtains, however. It has been claimed that at least one theatre in England had a safety curtain *before* 1887, and that may well be true, but at that time there was no law regarding their requirement. It is almost certain that the Exeter fire resulted in regulations being made, whereby safety curtains were a legal requirement in theatres of a certain seating capacity. It was also as a result of the disaster that a Fire Brigade was formed for the city. Until that time there had only been several small brigades dotted around the city and in outlying areas. So at least *some* good came from a horrific fatality.

It can only be hoped that as a result of the enquiry, sufficient lessons were to be learned by architects, planners, councils and others, to ensure that there would be little chance of such a tragedy happening again. Perhaps lessons were learned, for on December 17th, 1951 there *was* another fire at the Theatre Royal during the run-up to the pantomime *Babes in the Wood*. On this occasion

25. Fire engines at the scene of a fire at the theatre in 1951. Fortunately this was confined to a small area with only superficial damage. The fire was during the daytime, and in the run-up to the annual pantomime. There were no injuries.

the fire was restricted to an old paint room at the back of the stage. Although the Exeter Fire Brigade attended, the theatre staff had been able to bring the outbreak under control with suitable fire-fighting equipment installed in the stage area, so sadly lacking in the previous building. In 1951 the fire caused only minor damage to the structure, and whilst there were no injuries, local retired police officer John Tarr recalls that he was a motor patrol constable at the time, and attended the scene with a colleague. They entered the building and found one man unconscious as the result of smoke inhalation, but they were able to put their training as police officers to good use and successfully resuscitated him. The cause of the fire was never discovered.

In September 1887 fire had robbed the Exeter public of its theatre for a third time. Yet once again, like a Phoenix, another theatre arose from the sad ashes and remnants of what had been Exeter's fifth theatre. This improved, safer and more modern theatre would stand for over seventy years – and fire would not be the reason for the sixth theatre's ultimate fate.

THE GREAT THEATRE ROYAL FIRE. DEC 17TH 1951.

26. Local artist "Stil" produced this cartoon of the 1951 fire at the Theatre Royal. Virtually all the characters can be recognised including the then Mayor, Ald. Fred Cottey, and Cliff Gwilliam running from the left, Alfie Wills tripping over the hose, and Charlie Hutchings holding the ladder for Edward J. Wood. Stil's topical cartoons were part of the Exeter scene for many years.

The Architect

27. C.J. Phipps Esq. FSA, architect of many English theatres including the ill-fated Exeter Theatre Royal.

Charles John Phipps FSA, FRIBA, was born in Lansdowne, Bath in 1835. He started his career being articled to a firm of architects in Bath, but in 1858 he commenced on his own in that city. His design for the reconstruction of Bath Theatre (ironically after a disastrous fire there) was one of his early commissions, and after a few years he decided to move to London where he was to become an architect of note. He practiced in the capital until his death in 1897. It was said of Phipps that he was an architect "...who had made the building of theatres a special study, and had erected more than forty in London and various parts of the United Kingdom", although he was perhaps never as famous or as prolific as his contemporary, theatre architect Frank Matcham (born, incidentally, at Newton Abbot) – for Matcham designed close on 150 theatres in his life, including London's Hippodrome, Palladium and Coliseum.

Matcham was, perhaps, in a class of his own, but certainly Phipps must have run a close second. During his career, Phipps was advising architect to the Theatre Royal, Drury Lane for fifteen years, exhibitor of designs at the Royal Academy, and designer of various buildings including blocks of flats, business premises and hotels. He was one of the great Victorian theatre specialists, and was renowned as the acknowledged doyen in his field. His theatre designs often had a touch of classical architecture, and many of his buildings graced Victorian streets, standing out from neighbouring properties.

He was responsible for many fine civic buildings, and the architect of theatres such as London's *Gaiety, Shaftesbury, Comedy* and *Savoy*. The latter was said to have been one of the best he had designed, and was destined to become the home of the D'Oyly Carte Opera Company, itself famous for productions of Gilbert and Sullivan operettas. One of his last theatres, Her Majesty's in London's Haymarket, was completed just before his death in 1897.

28. The Savoy Opera House, London, one of Charles Phipps many theatre designs. For several decades it was the home of the D'Oyly Carte Opera Company.

Strange, then, that a man of so much experience, particularly in theatre design, should have apparently made so many errors at Exeter's Theatre Royal. Errors, according to Captain Shaw, that were directly responsible for the loss of so many lives. It would be impractical to go further regarding the findings of Captain Shaw. Questions must be asked, however, regarding the design of the

building. Why, for example, were exits constructed so as to be "cramped and tortuous"? Why were some of the passages and corridors within the building constructed of timber, lath and plaster, or matchboard, when the regulations stipulated fire-resisting materials? Why were walls, originally designed to be a minimum thirteen inches thick, in part only nine inches? Why did the design not include more exits, given that almost 1500 people could be in the audience on any given night? Why were some doors wooden and not made of fire-resisting metal?

Phipps had been somewhat indignant when it was suggested at the fire inquest that an iron curtain should have been available to shut off the stage from the auditorium. He retorted that it was not necessary and he knew of only one theatre in which such a device was available. He was also of the opinion that the building was safe, and that all the requirements of the regulations were met. When questioned about the scene-dock at the rear of the stage, Phipps dismissed that area as not being a scene dock, merely a storage space, and therefore need not have been separated from the stage in any way. During his evidence he insisted that a second exit from the gallery had been provided – yet it had most certainly not.

One other vitally important design fault, raised in the Fire Report, was the arrangement for lighting the stage and auditorium. Whilst the lights in various corridors, and other less important parts of the building were on one gas meter, the gas lighting for the stage was operated on the same meter as that of the auditorium. Thus, when it was necessary to shut off the gas supply to the stage lighting in an emergency – as indeed it was on the night of the fire – then the auditorium was also plunged into darkness. Why an experienced architect would not have insisted on separating these supplies is not known.

29. The third flight of stairs from the circle showing the pay box and a small door that hampered the exit of patrons.

Some of the points raised in Captain Shaw's report regarding design faults could in themselves seem, perhaps, quite innocuous, but they are not. When they are collated in such a report, they form a series of important errors which (and of this there can be little doubt) all contributed to the lightning-fast spread of the fire. These errors were, of course, the fault of the architect.

It has to be asked again, although the answer will never be known – why did Charles Phipps, if he was such an eminent architect of several theatres, make so many errors in his design of Exeter's Theatre Royal and how many other theatres in his design had similar faults? When he submitted his design in 1886, he was fifty-one years of age, and at the peak of his career. This was no young, inexperienced novice. This was no flippant person with scant regard for the outcome of his designs. This was a man with vast experience in designing buildings of all types and styles, and in particular the design of theatres. Such was Phipps' position within his professional field that his contemporaries looked upon him with great respect, acknowledging him as a man of great capabilities.

It is possible that Phipps designed the basic theatre building, but he may well have left much of the detail design to one of his staff, whilst he was engaged in other, perhaps more pressing, work. This theory may not have any accuracy, and certainly it was never mentioned in the fire report or at the Inquest. Yet it is a possibility, and even if an underling had made mistakes in design, would Phipps be prepared to admit his staff was at fault? Had he, perhaps, failed to double check work? It was bad enough that his own professional credibility was in question and being criticized; it would be understandable if Phipps chose not to have anyone else involved. Yet despite Phipps' apparent success, and despite his undoubted ability, mistakes he did make. Regrettably those were to contribute heavily towards the deaths of so many innocent people.

30. A scene depicting one of the funerals at the Higher Cemetery. In mass burials some coffins contained the remains of up six unidentified bodies.

The Coroner's Inquest

The Inquest was held at both The New London Inn and Guildhall, under the auspices of the Coroner, Henry W. Hooper Esq., sitting with Captain Shaw as his advisor.

There were many witnesses called. Some were asked to give their accounts of the fire, and to describe the grim picture of the interior. Others were called to explain how the building had been constructed, including anything they considered to be faults in design. Members of the public related how they assisted in removing bodies, both live and dead. Medical evidence was produced to show how intense the heat was to reduce many bodies to mere cinders. A local surgeon, Mr C. E. Bell, stated that whilst most victims had died as a result of severe burns, and others through suffocation by smoke, some had died as a result of severe scalding. He explained that the severity of the fire was such that any interior brick walls would have became so intensely hot, that as soon as any water hit them it would have turned to boiling hot vapour, scalding anyone nearby as it came off the walls.

After eight days, Mr Hooper submitted a long and detailed summing up. He explained to the jury their options, and asked them to retire and consider the points raised. The jury duly retired, and was out for over five hours. When they returned, they were unanimous in returning a verdict of accidental death. There was, of course, no other appropriate verdict. The jury's decision was correct, in that it was a tragic accident with devastating results.

The jury concluded that blame could not be apportioned to any person in particular. They were, however, extremely critical of the Licensing Magistrates, mainly for their failure in ensuring the necessary alterations, that should have been made prior to a licence being granted, had been carried out. Furthermore, they considered that the Magistrates had allowed themselves to be misled by the Architect with regard to a second exit from the gallery. Whilst shown on the architect's plans, and in spite of Phipps' insistence that there was a second exit, it had never been constructed.

They were critical of the arrangement on one staircase where a post interrupted the passage of people leaving, and where a pay box was badly sited. There had been a suggestion that on the original plans no such pay box was shown, and it is thought that it was included only after the Licensing Magistrates had made their inspection. There was also criticism of the lack of proper design for roof ventilation, contributing to the deaths of many people in the upper circle due to heat suffocation.

The seats in the gallery, at the back of the dress circles were at a slightly higher level than the auditorium ceiling. Smoke rising in the heat of the fire would have very quickly enveloped persons occupying them. The jury considered that the architect should have ensured the internal ceiling was considerably higher than the last row of public seating in the circle.

Referring to the lack of a second exit from the gallery, the jury rejected the architect's claim that there was a second means of escape in that patrons could have climbed over the gallery rail to the second circle. This, they pointed out, would have involved a drop of more than three feet and they expressed surprise that Mr Phipps should have even suggested it was feasible.

31. Robert Pople, proprietor of the New London Hotel, London Inn Square. He made his premises available for the injured and the stables for laying out bodies.

The jury severely criticized the architect, reiterating Captain Shaw's concern that Phipps, although considered a specialist, was able to produce a building with so many structural defects. They also considered the licensing magistrates discourteous by refusing to recognise both the authority of the Coroner's Court, and the Commissioner from the Government. In view of the criticisms levelled at the Magistrates, the Coroner had asked them to seek Counsel to act on their behalf, but they refused, appointing one of their number, a Mr Pengelly, to act for them as they had no intention of instructing Counsel.

The jury then made various proposals for improving safety in public buildings, such as the Chief Constable having power to visit such buildings unannounced, reporting to the Council regarding the availability and state of the emergency equipment in these building. They also recommended some form of water barrier or similar arrangement between the stage and auditorium.

Finally, and on a lighter note, the jury complained regarding the inability of jurors being able to take light refreshment during their deliberations. As the law prohibited this, they considered the law should be amended. On the suggestion of the Coroner, they decided not to include this as part of their verdict!

The Second Longbrook Street Theatre

The show, it is said, must go on; and go on it most certainly did. For just two years after the disastrous fire the Theatre Royal was able to open its doors once more. Reconstructed within the walls of the gutted former building, the new theatre boasted modern design construction, and improved facilities. Electricity was introduced, as was of course a safety curtain. To this day it remains a requirement that safety curtains are to be raised and lowered at least once during any public performance in theatres where more than 500 people can be accommodated, and this is why The Northcott and Barnfield Theatres in Exeter do not require one.

It is, of course, *this* building – the reconstructed Theatre Royal – that many readers will remember. It is this building also that was to dominate the theatrical scene in the City until the middle of the twentieth century. It is this building where our story really starts.

32. The rebuilt Theatre Royal, 1951. Yeoman of the Guard *(shown here during The Exeter Amateur Operatic Society production in 1951) was the show chosen by the D'Oyly Carte Company when the Theatre reopened in 1889.*

MISS IRENE VANBRUGH
AS LADY MARY LASENBY.

33. Locally-born Irene Vanburgh, one of two sisters who made their name in the world of theatre. In 1941 Irene was created a Dame for services to the theatre.

It cannot be said that the new Theatre Royal was anywhere near as ornate as its immediate predecessor. There were private boxes, with carpet and upholstered separate seating, but no swagged curtains. The cost of a private box was then three guineas – a large sum for that period. The front of the circle was quite plain, without the attractive plasterwork relief and designs included in the original circle. Its only adornment was a red velvet top, with a round brass handrail covering the entire length. There was a circular domed ceiling, but not as large as that in the previous auditorium. There were, however, attractive pastel murals in each segment of the dome. The large plaster reliefs that had covered the original walls were now replaced by huge oil paintings. Whilst it may not have been as attractive on the inside as the former theatre, it was certainly safer, with much more use of brick and concrete in the construction. There were far more exits and much improved lighting. More importantly, far better provisions for fire fighting had been provided. Safety was of utmost importance in the redesigned building. Had a similar fire broken out, which thankfully did not happen, it is almost certain that the improvements would have prevented anything like the huge death toll of 1887.

The Theatre opened in October, 1879 with a performance of *The Yeomen of the Guard* by the famous D'Oyly Carte company. (Ironically, of course, their London home was The Savoy Opera House – designed by the architect Charles Phipps!) For the next seventy years and more the Theatre Royal, Longbrook Street, was set to become, for many, almost part of family life. The *Exeter Flying Post* reported that there was "not a seat unoccupied". It went on to say: "The scene in the circle, filled with ladies and gents in evening dress, was exceedingly bright and gay. Punctually at eight o'clock, the Titancrete curtain rose slowly and disclosed a magnificent painting of a scene on Dartmoor, which forms the Act Drop. Mr Widgery's effective picture is surrounded by a handsome border designed by Mr Alfred Darbyshire, and painted by Mr James Sidney". The Widgery referred to was Mr William Widgery, a renowned local artist and father of F. J. Widgery, sometime Mayor of Exeter. Mr James Sidney was the theatre's scenic artist.

The paper also mentions that the external appearance was enhanced by the addition of some fine shrubs at the escape portico – the shrubs being the gift of Mr Sclater of the Alexandra Nursery, the long established Exeter nursery.

The report also pointedly mentioned "the floors of the pit and circle are of Titancrete, and the stairs of concrete". It added that "where the occupants of the Theatre have to place their feet in making their way out are completely unburnable". On a more technical note, the paper mentioned "the house is lighted by electricity in a most effective manner… the current under control from the prompt side, by switches mounted on a polished granite slate". These comments were obviously included to assure the public that the new theatre had been designed with safety in mind.

In the early days of theatre, it was not uncommon for patrons – then often standing in the pit area – to voice their approval or otherwise in various ways. Actors who were less well received could expect heckling as the minimum; frequently objects were thrown on stage, and fights would break out within the audience, probably causing more interest for a few minutes than the show itself! Over the passing years, however, audiences became more restrained,

34. Both Irene and Violet Vanburgh appeared at the theatre. Violet is shown playing the lead role in a 1911 play.

hissing and shouting becoming virtually reserved for pantomime. For example, children would shout a warning whenever the *Demon King* appeared on stage, and would loudly warn someone of danger lurking behind. An evening at the Theatre became an outing for many – especially those who came from quite some distance to see the latest offering from the 'Royal'. Many touring companies were still regular visitors, particularly in the war years, when many London theatres were closed. Such companies would attract what was then called 'charabancs', now known as coaches, bringing patrons from outlying areas.

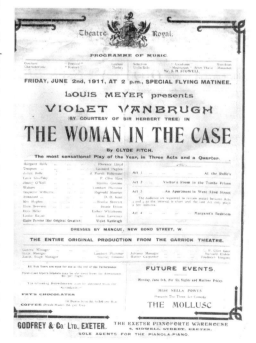

Hippodrome, Exeter
Grand Anniversary

Monday, November 6th

Special

Souvenir ..

Programme

36. Exeter born Fred Karno became a legend in the world of theatre. He is seen pictured here in his souvenir programme for the Exeter Hippodrome, which he owned for 10 years.

Early notables to grace the stage in Longbrook Street included Sir Henry Irving, Ben Greet, Fred Karno and the locally-born sisters Violet and Irene Vanburgh. Henry Irving, the first English actor to be knighted, spent his latter years as manager of London's Lyceum Theatre, but had been noted for his Shakespearean successes, frequently with Ellen Terry as his leading lady.

Violet Vanburgh was born in 1867, the eldest daughter of the Revd Reginald and Frances Barnes. Reverend Barnes was the vicar of Heavitree and a friend of Sir Henry Irving. When in London he would take his children to The Lyceum, and make use of Irving's private box. It was as a result of such theatre visits that Violet became smitten and decided to take acting as her career. During her early acting days, she lodged in London with the actress Ellen Terry who suggested she change her name from Barnes to Vanburgh. She later married Arthur Bourchier who was at one time manager of The Garrick theatre in London. Violet died in 1942 and was buried at Stoke Canon.

Irene Vanburgh was born in 1872, and like her sister was educated at Exeter High School, now The Maynard. After many local amateur appearances, she too decided on a theatrical career and became a professional actress in 1888. Irene played most theatres in London, and frequently toured, sometimes abroad. She made several appearances at the Theatre Royal, the last in 1945 as Lady Stanhope in *She Sleeps Lightly.* Both Irene and Violet were fortunate to have worked alongside such personalities as George Alexander, Herbert Beerbohm Tree, John Hare, Henry Irving, Sir Charles Wyndham and, of course,

36. Sir Henry Irving, one of the finest actors of the 19th century stage, and manager of the Lyceum Theatre, London. The Vanburgh family had use of his private box at that theatre.

CHAS·A·BUCHEL
MR. H. B. IRVING as CRICHTON.

Arthur Bourchier. Irene was created a Dame in 1941, a few years before her death in 1949.

Fred Karno was born in Exeter in 1866, the son of a local cabinet maker, and christened Frederick Westcott. He was for many years the owner of the Hippodrome in London Inn Square, later The Plaza. Karno was to reach considerable heights in the world of theatre, making many friends in the entertainment world, notably in Hollywood. He helped many young and sometimes struggling actors in their careers, including Charlie Chaplin, Stan Laurel (of Laurel & Hardy fame), Robb Wilton, Max Miller and many others. Karno also ventured into various business deals, and at one stage purchased property in Camberwell, London, where he created his "fun factory". Here he constructed a scene dock, wardrobe store and props room, wrote pantomimes and devised sketches. In the 1914 pantomime *Mother Goose* at the Theatre Royal, the scenery was billed as being "from Fred Karno's studios".

Names of all the famous people who appeared at Exeter during the Theatre Royal's existence would take far too much space to reproduce. Many are

37. Gertrude Ford who played Fairy Goodheart in Percy Dunsford's Dick Whittington *in 1924.*

included later, but the likes of Randolph Sutton, Noel Coward, Jack Buchanan, Alistair Sim, Ellie Shields, Wee Georgie Wood, Clarkson Rose, Tommy Trinder, Henry Hall, Arthur Askey, Lupino Lane and many, many others have all walked the boards at the Royal at some time; all were household names and much respected artists. Each and every one could be the subject of a chapter, if not a book itself. Indeed many have been the subject of biographies, including Fred Karno.

Every year we witness the passing of actors and actresses who have, during their careers in the often unstable world of theatre, given the public the best that they could offer. From unknown artists, perhaps appearing for the first time, to large multi-cast productions; from solo singers to huge chorus numbers; from comedies to Shakespearean dramas – the 'Royal' provided a temporary haven for them all; and it could be claimed that nowhere was pantomime more enthusiastically received than in Exeter.

Theatres, like all corporate bodies, thrive on good management and loyal staff. Perhaps, in the latter years of the Royal, the management could have been more forward looking – but many of the staff remained loyal to the bitter end. How bitter that ending must have seemed for some. For it was in Longbrook Street that many established their second home.

Theatre is a peculiar being. It can be warm and kind, yet distant and unfriendly. It can be rewarding yet a hard taskmaster. For those whose very existence it is, it becomes a vital part of living, in the blood, and a daily – often nightly – routine unlike any other occupation. Who, normally, would want to spend almost every evening in a world of make-believe where often one works in virtual darkness, frequently unable to talk in normal tones and often ignored by those who, without such people in the background, would not have been able to achieve fame or glory? Such is the life of those backstage or front-of-house. Always present, but seldom were they considered. Yet there has always been that *something* that attracted and allured people to the stage. In this respect, theatre has not really changed over the years.

There are many names written in the Theatre Royal history that could claim to have been loyal to that institution during its existence in the City. Probably the most talked about person was PERCY DUNSFORD – a name almost synonymous with the Royal. In 1897 he began his days in Longbrook Street under the then manager, a Mr Gault. Percy stayed at the Theatre until his death in 1940, by which time he had become the manager.

In 1909 Percy Dunsford realised the public appeal of pantomime. He advised the Theatre directors to produce their own pantomimes, and it was from that year that the Theatre started to do so. Shortly afterwards, Percy was asked to take over the productions. It was largely for his pantomime success that Percy Dunsford will be remembered, and indeed it was thanks to Percy, and later Cliff Gwilliam, that Exeter can be justly proud of its seventy-three consecutive pantomimes.

Over the years, such productions were to give children so much pleasure. Children, perhaps, of all ages! For was it *really* just the children who wanted to go to "the panto", or was it Mum and Dad who were even more eager?

For many years Percy, or "Uncle Percy" as most children came to know him, wrote a Children's Letter in the pantomime programme. Fond of children and liking nothing more than meeting them and shaking their hands, he created a wonderful atmosphere of mystery and surprise at "panto time", encouraging children to sign his special book, entitled *Uncle Percy's Pantomime Album*.

In this book children wrote their names and addresses, together with their age at the time of their visit. Looking through one of these albums today, one can find a host of local people who signed their names, and innocently put their age alongside. How some must now regret doing that!

Even more interesting in the albums is the record of people visiting from far afield. Often a number of children from places many miles distant have signed the same page, suggesting that they were in one of the many coach-parties that attended each pantomime. Uncle Percy died in 1940 at the age of 63, but even today his memory lingers with many local people.

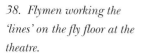

38. Flymen working the 'lines' on the fly floor at the theatre.

EDWARD J. WOOD was another 'personality'. He will probably always be remembered for his *Demon* or *King Rat* parts. Official photographs often showed him with trilby hat and bow tie. A somewhat less fearsome image, perhaps, than if one encountered him between pantomime performances, leaving the stage door in Longbrook Street for his home in nearby Poltimore Square – still in full demon make-up! Very un-professional, but that was "Woodie". He first came to the Theatre Royal as a member of Frank Benson's Shakespearean company. Not only

39. Cliff Gwilliam, manager of the theatre. Appointed in 1945, he remained as manager until it closed in 1962.

did he later take part in many of the post-war pantomimes, he was, under Cliff Gwilliam, associate producer of many. He was also the Theatre stage director for many years.

CLIFF GWILLIAM was a name immediately and automatically associated with the post-war years. Resplendent in evening dress, he was frequently to be seen in the foyer before performances greeting his patrons. A very upright figure, his 'trademark' was a large Havana-type cigar. Seemingly never without one, it was usual to see him in person, or photograph, in a *Churchillian* pose. For the local cartoonist "Stil", Cliff Gwilliam was a perfect character. Portly, horn-rimmed spectacles, receding hair, evening dress, cigar – what more could a cartoonist wish?

Cliff was almost born into the entertainment world. A musician of some ability, his younger days saw him playing in various orchestras. Later he was to form his own, touring not only England but also the continent. Following a brief spell in military service, Cliff was to join the Odeon Cinema organisation. He was quickly successful, and became a cinema manager for the Odeon chain.

It was during his term as manager of Exeter's Odeon cinema (opened in Sidwell Street in 1937) that he was to be enticed 'down the road'. In 1945 the directors of the Theatre approached Cliff Gwilliam and offered him the position as manager of the Theatre Royal. Cliff Gwilliam accepted, and the appointment was approved on 19th May 1945, at a board meeting under the chairmanship of Rowland Glave Saunders, who was Mayor of Exeter during most of the war years.

Cliff Gwilliam managed the Theatre in the grand, traditional manner of 'impresario'. No doubt this style would not be possible today, but that was Cliff Gwilliam. He loved spectacle. He knew what the public wanted and tried to provide it if at all possible. Above all he wanted his patrons to enjoy *their* Theatre, and tried to ensure that their every visit was a night out, and something that they could enthuse about afterwards. TCG – as Cliff Gwilliam was frequently known by the theatre staff – would no doubt have managed the Theatre until he retired, had not the premises been sold in 1962. After its closure, he moved from Exeter and took positions in Ringwood, Taunton and Torquay before his death in 1970, aged just 67. For many who visited the Theatre during his term as manager, Cliff will best be remembered as he frequently appeared in Stil's cartoons.

EDMUND GAETON became the Musical Director of the Theatre Royal orchestra in 1934. Although he had held similar positions at Bristol and Leicester, he was no stranger to the Royal. From 1921 he wrote the music for Percy Dunsford's pantomimes. When he and his family moved from Leicester, and were looking for a suitable house, they accepted Percy's invitation to stay with him at 'Panorama', his home in Pennsylvania.

The name 'Edmund Gaeton' is slightly misleading, as it was a stage name. His surname was, in fact, Edmund. 'Geyton' was a family Christian name. By simply changing the spelling of that, and putting his surname first, he gave himself the infinitely more theatrical name of *Edmund Gaeton*. Furthermore, on occasions the intrigue was enhanced when he added an *umlaut* to the letter 'e' of the already Teutonic sounding name of *Gaeton*. One reason for this was that it was generally considered during the twenties and thirties that German musicians were more credible. This backfired on him at the outset of the Second World War, although he retained his stage name without the umlaut!

Unlike most Theatre Royal personalities, Edmund Gaeton was not instantly recognisable – but that is, perhaps, not surprising when he spent most of his working life in the orchestra pit with his back to the audience, with only the rear of his head and shoulders visible to the public! Edmund Gaeton continued as the Theatre's Musical Director until 1953, when the orchestra was disbanded as a permanent unit. He had conducted many musicians in the depths of the orchestra pit, and some of those could possibly still be playing today. He died in 1969 aged 77.

This is perhaps the most appropriate place to mention the orchestra. For many years the nucleus of the Theatre Royal Orchestra was constant, and several members also played in the surrounding area. Orchestras for local amateur operatic societies were almost guaranteed to contain at least one or two members from the Theatre Royal, assuming that they were not required in Exeter at that time. Others played for small dance bands or for one-off musical events held in the area. Some well-known Exeter musicians were regulars in the Theatre Royal orchestra for many years – Stowell, Wellsman, Huxham, Peache and many others. Often they stayed for many years as, for example did

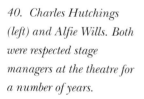

40. Charles Hutchings (left) and Alfie Wills. Both were respected stage managers at the theatre for a number of years.

Jimmy Welsman, a clarinetist, and Ernie Peache the percussionist. Some families had more than one member in the orchestra (the Huxhams and Wellsmans spring to mind); others, such as the Peache family, had husband in the orchestra and wife front of house. Quite a family orientated theatre at times! Ernie Peache was also a talented poster writer for the Theatre, and also operated the lift at Colsons (now Dingles) store in High Street for many years.

The disbandment of the orchestra was largely financial, but partly resulted from the directors installing an organ towards the end of the Theatre's life. Early in 1953 a decision was taken that a full orchestra was not required, and four of the nine resident musicians were given notice. As a result, there followed the one and only strike at the Theatre Royal. The musicians who had been retained objected to their colleagues being dismissed, and refused to play until they were reinstated. Cliff Gwilliam ignored their demands, and was backed by his fellow directors in the matter.

At first it seemed just a minor dispute, but turned into something far more serious. In order to provide the necessary musical content in many shows, Gwilliam arranged for non-union musicians to form an orchestra, and that of course only inflamed the situation. The Musicians Union became deeply involved and prohibited any member to play at the Theatre Royal. It seems hard to believe that the dispute even reached the dizzy heights of Westminster! When Cliff Gwilliam arranged for three or four musicians from the then Devonshire Regiment to augment his temporary orchestra (the regimental headquarters being at Topsham Barracks), questions were asked in the House whether that was against War Office regulations. Army musicians did not come within the scope of the Musicians Union, but obviously the Government was somewhat concerned that their use in such a way could be contentious. Stalemate existed for over twelve months, but eventually the orchestra as a permanent, resident team was disbanded, and subsequent orchestras were to be formed for the shows requiring accompanying music, under the baton of various musical directors including Terance Casey and Walter B. Smith.

There were many more people connected with the general running of the Theatre but whom it is impossible to name. The doormen and usherettes, who assisted thousands of patrons over the years, became more than just employees for many people. Regulars got to know them, and they became familiar faces. In fact it was only the front-of-house staff who were seen by the patrons. Backstage workers were (hopefully!) never seen. Ice cream and programme sellers, the cafe staff, cleaners, maintenance persons – all could be

41. Blackie, the theatre cat. Having strayed into the theatre during a pantomime run, Blackie made his home backstage, and no doubt kept down the mice in the building!

staff who often 'doubled' in other Theatre jobs, and were so vital to the day-to-day running of the Theatre. Although few could match Alfie Wills' incredible length of service at the theatre, many staff worked there for over 30 years, including front-of-house employees Louisa Serpentelli (always known as "Serpie") who looked after patrons in the circle and also worked in the circle bar, Edith Swinford, and Violet Downing.

42. Percy Dunsford pre-war manager of the theatre. He produced many fine pantomimes and encouraged children to sign 'Uncle Percy's Album'.

For many years the box-office team was headed by Miss Mogridge, and later by Marjorie Meadows (also secretary to Cliff Gwilliam), during an era where everything was, of course pre-computer. Reservations, cancellations, and issuing of tickets were manual operations. Errors could easily be made, but such was their efficiency that seldom was there any serious problem. In the box office was a small model of the interior of the theatre, showing each seat numbered. Thus it was possible at the time of booking to choose the exact seat required, assuming it was available. Many booked the same seats each time they visited the theatre. Furthermore, the majority of reservations were by cash. Cheques were not commonplace, and of course 'plastic money', the credit card, was unheard of. Administration was hard work, with no easy way out! Whilst much modern theatre booking in Exeter is computer orientated, there are still several instances where manual booking systems are in operation. Technology has not quite taken over completely!

Those backstage were never in the limelight as were Percy Dunsford, Cliff Gwilliam and others. Even so, one or two names have become almost legends in the local theatrical world despite being unseen by the general public.

For many years, Miss EDDIE PEARCE was wardrobe mistress for Exeter pantomimes, and responsible for some outstanding creations. Another lady, much loved by those who had the pleasure of knowing her, was Peggy MacQueen. Peggy had been a professional wardrobe mistress with the D'Oyly Carte Opera Company, and later in her career assisted in the creation of the fabulous costumes for Percy Dunsford's pantomimes. A charming lady with a delightful personality, Peggy continued working into her 'retirement' years, helping to dress shows for local amateur groups. Her ability and professional approach to even an amateur production was pure dedication. Peggy MacQueen died in 1976.

Latterly Alfie Wills and Charles Hutchings were joint stage managers at the Theatre, and were almost a double act in themselves! Alfie and Charlie were two of life's gentlemen. Their knowledge of things theatrical would have been difficult to surpass locally. Between them, over many years, they led a team of dedicated people – the majority of whom had a great feeling for the Theatre. Some were full-time employees, some part-time staff and others merely helped out on a casual basis, as and when the need arose. For pantomime and larger shows, the back-stage team would be considerable; but more of that later.

There are, today, several people in Exeter who worked behind the scenes at the Royal, playing some part in ensuring the smooth transformation from one scene to another. Since the last war they worked under the auspices of Alfie Wills, Charles Hutchings or more recently, David Edmund.

ALFIE WILLS began his career at the Theatre Royal in 1904. He started as a programme seller – when programmes cost threepence, or slightly more than 1p in today's currency! Following one or two other comparatively menial positions he was appointed Property Master. This was – and still is in today's theatre – a most responsible job backstage. He became an assistant stage manager under the stage director, Reggie Crowe, and was appointed Stage Manager in 1917, and remained until 1952. For an incredible thirty-five years Alfie was the 'boss' of the stage and, because he knew his job so well, was a most respected and popular Stage Manager, not just locally, but throughout the Country. The number of Christmas cards he received at the Theatre each year would vouch for that. Alfie's latter years were spent in conjunction with Charles Hutchings – simply because an unfortunate hearing problem made it difficult for him to work as efficiently as he would have liked. It was because of this that Alfie gave up the position as Stage Manager in 1952 and handed over the reins to Charles Hutchings. Alfie then became House Manager, taking him from behind the scenes to the opposite end of the Theatre. Even so, there remained a close liaison between the two. Alfie Wills stayed as House Manager until the theatre's closure, and he died in the same year. Those who worked backstage will remember *Blackie*, the cat 'adopted' by Alfie when it strayed into the Theatre one day during a pantomime performance, and stayed there.

CHARLES HUTCHINGS took over from Alfie and remained Stage Manager until he retired in 1956. Charles was one of a family who were much involved in backstage life.

His brother, Dick, worked part-time, mainly for matinees. His uncle, Tommy, was a full-time employee and worked the main curtain, or house tabs. Thus, when the main curtain

43. For many years stage director, Edward J. Wood had a small part in the theatre's annual panto-mime.

44. Edward J. Wood in costume for his role as 'Major Domo' in the production of Cinderella *in 1958/9.*

45. Edmund Gaeton became musical director of the theatre in 1934 and remained until 1953. For many years he wrote much of the music for the annual pantomime.

46. A newspaper vendor in High Street. The poster advertises the musicians' strike in 1953. Despite the strike, the theatre's resident orchestra was later disbanded.

rose, it would have been Tommy hauling it up manually – hand over hand on a thick hemp rope. Charles also had a brother, Bert, who worked part time when required.

Charlie had been the stage carpenter, and at one time the property master, but accepted the position of joint Stage Manager when Alfie Wills started to have hearing problems. Although he was not the Stage Manager for as many years as Alfie Wills, Charlie Hutchings was given the same respect as his predecessor, for his ability and knowledge was on a par. He spent many hours helping out with amateur shows, and was a quiet, humorous man. On retiring as Stage Manager, Charles was succeeded by David Edmund – who in turn retained that position until the Theatre closed in 1962. Charles Hutchings died some ten years later.

DAVID EDMUND worked for many years at the Theatre Royal. The son of the Musical Director, Edmund Gaeton, David started his career in the theatre as a young man. During his National Service the drama club at R.A.F. Yatesbury used him as their electrician and lighting designer. He was later to work in a similar capacity with many amateur companies. At the Theatre Royal, he was an electrician, later Chief Electrician, and eventually Stage Manager.

Having worked with Alfie Wills and Charles Hutchings for many years, it was inevitable that David was to become a fountain of knowledge backstage. He was meticulous and a professional, expecting his team to be similarly professional in their stage work – even if they were only brought in for the occasional show. Always mindful of the fact that on the other side of the curtain was the public, who had paid to see the best, David had no time for slackness or incompetence on stage. He encouraged and assisted anyone new to this strange backstage world, and was always happy to explain how things were done – even down to how certain knots should be tied, or how certain pieces of scenery should be secured. He was forever in demand by the amateur societies, and for many years was Stage Manager for the local Societies of Exmouth, Dawlish, Teignmouth, Tiverton, Axminster and elsewhere.

47. Peter J. Jarman, theatre critic of the Express & Echo.

As the last Stage Manager at the theatre, his final 'production' was to assemble all the lots on stage in readiness for the auctioneers after the Theatre had closed its doors. Having been responsible for staging so many 'happenings' at the Theatre, some good and others perhaps not so good, that job must have been quite strange, for the livelihood that he, and his family, had known for so many year, was about to disappear.

They may have all now departed this life, but the names of Alfie Wills, Charlie Hutchings and David Edmund will long be remembered with great respect and affection.

One other person, although not an employee of the Theatre, should also be mentioned. Not an actor, musician, or stagehand, indeed not in any way connected with the Theatre apart from his occupation. He was, though, almost as much a part of the Theatre Royal's recent history as any other person, and has to be included within this story. Such was his personality, he was usually referred to by just his three initials – *P.J.J.*

PETER J. JARMAN was the film and drama critic of the *Express & Echo* in Exeter. He started a journalistic career in Tiverton and after the second War returned there until 1948, when he joined the staff of the *Express & Echo*.

P. J. J. was became an acknowledged expert on the film industry, and a keen follower of the professional and amateur theatre, seldom missing a local performance. An articulate person, and fascinating character, his knowledge of the theatre and film world gave him a host of stories and anecdotes to relate. He had met and knew personally many 'stars' of the two industries, in particular the film star Deanna Durbin, for whom he had much admiration. His love of horror films led him to become friends with Peter Cushing and Boris Karloff. He spent over 21 years as a reporter for the *Express & Echo*, and during that time interviewed scores of people who were, or went on to become, household names.

In an article for the *Express & Echo*, David Edmund recalled PJJ reviewing a variety show at the Theatre Royal in 1950. In his review, Jarman picked out a couple whom, he thought, 'had something which should make them big successes'. The then young and comparatively inexperienced Morecombe and Wise went on to prove him so right! Regularly in his pantomime reviews, PJJ enthused with remarks such as those for the 1953 *Dick Whittington*, when he praised 'the glossy costumes, the scenes splashed vividly with colour and the captivating lights of worlds far from here'. His regular reports on shows produced by local companies seldom contained any severe criticism, for Peter was reluctant to be *too* critical unless it was totally unavoidable. He knew well that performers could sometimes lack the sparkle expected of them, for even the most hardened performer can be nervous, and newcomers can often have trouble with stage-fright. Nevertheless, he would encourage them rather than destroy them. In particular he encouraged amateurs in what, after all, was their hobby. He had a love of, and a feeling for, the theatre, which made it difficult for him to be harsh on those whom he considered were doing the best they could.

At times, however, he did criticise. In 1952 his review of the play *Friendly Relations* reported that the domestic comedy 'had its weaknesses'. After leaving Exeter, the play was to start its London run. Peter Jarman suggested that before doing so 'something should be done about the rambling trivialities of the first thirty minutes'. Mainly, however, PJJ, was more appreciative. In November 1961 he reviewed the play *No Time for Love*, saying he could not entirely agree with the title because he thought readers would 'love the show and every adorable character in it'! In that same year he appeared almost spellbound by the performances of Cicely Courtneidge, Jack Hulbert and Robertson Hare in *The Bride Comes Back*. 'They have', he said, 'combined talents not to be ignored'. His report of the show includes the words 'sparkle', 'gloss', 'polish', and he sums it all up as 'wonderful entertainment'.

Peter Jarman was a journalist of the old school, who also lamented the passing of the Theatre Royal, for this had been a virtual second home to him. A charming person, he was one of those characters never forgotten. Sadly, in October 1969, Peter Jarman suffered a sudden brain haemorrhage whilst reviewing a show at what was the Riverside Club in Okehampton Street. He died a fortnight later, at the age of only 45.

48. Box Office staff preparing for the 1953 pantomime Dick Whittington. *On the left is Miss Mogridge with Mrs Goldsworthy answering the telephone.*

49. Reg Varney who appeared in Sky High *at the theatre in 1951. The show had previously been a hit at the London Palladium.*

Famous Artistes at Exeter

Over the years – from the very early days of theatre in the city to date – there has been a constant flow of 'names' appearing at the various theatres here. Some were already famous, and others in their early days.

Obviously as time passes, those who can recall the early days at Longbrook Street are becoming fewer. There is, of course, no person living now who can recall the Theatre Royal before the start of the twentieth century. However, there are probably scores of people who can recall the comparative recent times. Dozens of names from the 1930s, 1940s and 1950s would bring back memories for many; names that would be a touch of nostalgia for those who regularly visited the theatre, listened to radio, or had the opportunity of watching early television. In later pages the names of several who took part in pantomimes have been recalled, but during the remainder of each year there were many other shows featuring well-known personalities of the day.

From the years before and after the Second World War there is an abundance of personalities who were household names. Many had their own catchphrases – for

50. Dame Anna Neagle who played in More the merrier *at Exeter in 1960.*

example Arthur Askey's 'Hello Playmates' or Jimmy Wheeler's 'Ay Ay, that's yer lot'. Some will be remembered by a certain song – as in Cavan O'Connor's *I'm only a strolling Vagabond*. Others were known by physical peculiarities in their acts. Jimmy James had a certain way of smoking his cigar, and Norman Evans possessed an incredible 'rubber' face, emulated more recently by Les Dawson. Many, of course, were just themselves and needed nothing more than to walk on stage to ensure a round of applause. A classic example of this was Jimmy James' partner Eli, who rarely stuttered more than a word or two, but could stand on stage looking the complete gormless idiot and create instant humour. Tommy Cooper only had to walk on and look around to make his audience cry with laughter. Today, the likes of Freddie Starr possess a similar ability.

The Theatre Royal handbills, distributed to advertise the weekly shows, bring back evocative memories of the various plays and variety shows seen there. On these can be found the names of the well known, and the lesser known. Some of the then lesser known, of course, could have risen to greater things and perhaps eventually appeared at the top of a billing. It must have been of great personal satisfaction for an artiste to see his or her name climb up that ladder of public acknowledgement, finally reaching the top. Consider just a few of the names who 'trod the boards' in Longbrook Street over the past fifty or sixty years.

Gillie Potter, who first introduced his Marshmellow family of Hogsnorton at an Exeter pantomime in 1926; Hutch, with that wonderful voice; Suzette Tarri, an early comedienne; Henry Hall and his famous orchestra; Bransby Williams who, aged over 80, was still an acknowledged one man show; Ronald Shiner, who produced and appeared in shows here; Michael Miles and his Radio Forfeits game; Stainless Stephen; Sonnie Hale; Morris & Cowley, the

RADIO TIMES July 25, 1947

HENRY HALL'S GUEST NIGHT

at 7.0 this evening is the last of the present series and will come from the stage of the Theatre Royal, Exeter

\- 9 -

Time to say goodnight — AH+C.

HENRY HALL: (Cont'd) This is Henry Hall speaking just to say goodbye for now and "Here's to the Next time".

"Here's to the next time" Chappell

ANNOUNCER: You have been listening to Henry Hall's Guest Night from the Theatre Royal, Exeter. Henry Hall and his orchestra go on holiday at the end of this week and will resume their Guest Night programmes on September 2nd.

25th July, 1947
BL/MJW

52. In 1947 'Henry Hall's Guest Night' came from the stage of the theatre. The Radio Times programme advert and the last page of the programme script are shown above.

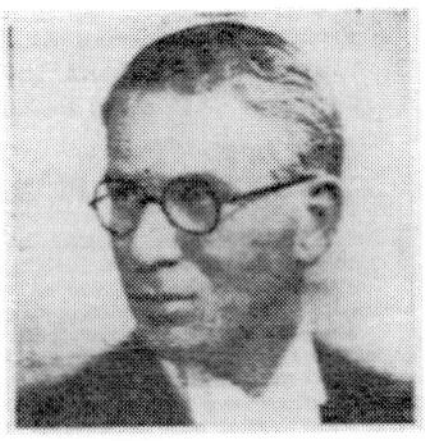

comedians; Monsewer Eddie Gray; Wally Patch; Sid Milward and the Nitwits; Cyril Fletcher, famous for his 'odd odes'.

The lovable purveyors of gossip Gert & Daisy (Elsie and Doris Waters); pianist Carroll Gibbons; those cads The Western Brothers, who were both locally; the voice of them all Peter Cavanagh; Jessie Matthews; Beryl Reid; singers Anne Zeigler & Webster Booth; Ethel Revnell; Cardew 'the Cad' Robinson; Turner Layton; Reg Varney – who was at Exeter as long ago as 1951; Jack Train & Anona Winn, both also of 'Twenty Questions' fame.

The trumpeter Nat Gonella; Ted Heath and his orchestra; Ella Shields of 'Burlington Bertie' fame; the vast Fred Emney; the Kordites singing group; the tenor Monte Rey; Hattie Jacques, probably more remembered for the 'Carry On' films; Issy Bonn; Albert and Les Ward; and the hugely popular George Formby. The list really is endless, and others have already been mentioned elsewhere. Many more names of equal importance and popularity could be added, but those mentioned are probably enough to stir the imagination!

Apart from the weekly shows and short runs, the Theatre also staged one-off events. Sunday concerts were often held, which could mean an appearance of the Black Watch Band, the Torquay Municipal orchestra, or perhaps a quartet of local singers. In June 1950 the Vancouver Boys Band gave a Sunday concert. Also on Sundays, the Theatre staged what was known as Pleasant Sunday Afternoons, or People's Sunday Afternoons, more often abbreviated to simply P.S.A. Well attended, the afternoon concerts helped boost the Theatre's finances. There are numerous other events that could be mentioned, but some just have to be left out.

Ballet was also a popular event, and visiting companies have included the Sadler's Wells, Ballet Rambert, the Allied Ballet and Continental Ballet. As happens today, the dance programme changed daily. This of course entailed different sets, costumes and music for each day, and thus it was not just the dancers who were kept on their toes! The theatre stage was constructed of softwood planking. During normal wear and tear over the years, as the timber was worn down, any knots in the wood, being harder, were left slightly raised. It was therefore often necessary for the floor to be sanded flat before ballet dancers could perform safely.

Pantomime

Pantomime! An event so very British, it is difficult for any other nation to appreciate how enthusiastically it is received in the British Isles.

It is only in comparatively recent times that pantomime – *panto* as we now tend to call it – has been traditionally a Christmas show, often opening a few days before that festivity. It is now more usual for a pantomime to open on

53. Pantomime Programme for Mother Goose, *1932, featuring Saxon Davis in the title role.*

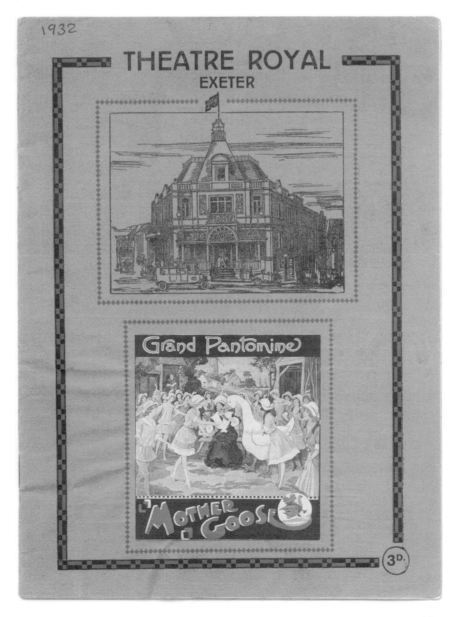

Boxing Day, and it can run for several weeks, particularly in the larger theatres of London and other major cities. For many years pantomime has been the time of year when theatres engage 'stars' in the major roles – and theatres, naturally, will compete against each other for the best box-office attractions. It should be, of course, a guaranteed income for possibly two or more months, and pantomime is therefore a welcome ingredient of the theatre's existence. In 1877, a newspaper report in *The Graphic* claimed that 'pantomime was dying because of the marvelous complexity of mechanism, painting, limelight, coloured fire and ballet girls'. How fortunate it is that the report was to prove so wrong in its prediction. For pantomime is very much alive today, and still attracting large numbers of patrons to theatres all over the country.

Exeter always had a very much respected and well-attended pantomime, and like other theatres in provincial cities, the Theatre Royal ensured that 'big names' from all over the country were retained to take both lead roles and supporting parts. Today it is commonplace for stars of sport and television to take lead parts in the larger pantomimes, but that is comparatively modern practice. For many years it had been normal for the stars and acts in pantomime to be taken from within the acting profession. There were certainly enough popular artistes to go around, and some have already been mentioned. In the years before the Second World War, the likes of Hay Plumb, Beryl Seton, Albert H. Grant, Enid Lowe, George Lacy and Saxon Davis would attract audiences not only at Exeter, but also in theatres all over the country. Shortly after the war, Albert Whelan, Gillie Potter, Jean Sweetman, Fred McNaughton and Betty Lotinga were just a few of the long list of popular pantomime names to appear in the city.

54. Cissie Thompson played principal boy Colin in Mother Goose *at the Exeter pantomime in 1914/15, and Robin Hood in* Babes in the Wood *the following year.*

In view of the fact that Exeter was at the forefront of pantomime productions for several decades, it is perhaps right to reflect on this annual event. It must be remembered that in Exeter, more than any other place, pantomime was one part of the whole theatre spectrum for which the theatre management could be justifiably proud. For the Theatre Royal still holds the record for a consecutive run of annual pantomimes – a total of seventy-three at the close. This will doubtless stand for many years to come, and is an achievement for a provincial theatre.

Even the smallest village will stage a pantomime. For months before, local enthusiasts will set about writing the story, composing the odd song or two and constructing the set. There are always people in a village who will, albeit often reluctantly, appear on stage; and there are always those who enjoy making themselves look fools in front of their fellow residents. One always knows who the Dame will be, and one also finds out very quickly who the *prima donnas* will be!

Historically, it is difficult to pinpoint the beginning of pantomime. Theatre historians have traced origins back to the sixteenth and seventeenth centuries. Indeed, some will argue that Roman mime of some 2000 years ago was probably the true origin. It is generally accepted that pantomime has its roots in Italian comedy. Certainly this is a strong probability, since it is known that Italian actors appeared in this country around the beginning of the seventeenth century. In the very early part of the eighteenth century the word 'pantomime' appeared on London playbills, and over the following decades our traditional pantomime has evolved.

As early as December 1869 a pantomime at the second Bedford Circus Theatre was advertised in the *Devon Weekly Times*:

> *On Friday, 24th December will be produced the Grand Comic Christmas Pantomime of 'Number Nip' or 'Harlequin and the Gnome King of the Giant Mountains', with entirely new and gorgeous scenery by Mr H. Caprani and assistants. Masks, dresses and mechanical effects by Messrs Fawdon, Moxey, and Wiltstone.*
>
> *Harlequin: Mons. C. Massoni.*
>
> *Columbine: Miss Rose Graham.*
>
> *Clown: Dan Rice.*
>
> *Pantaloon: Mr McCabe.*
>
> *Morning performances on Monday December 27th and Friday 31st at Two o'clock.*
>
> *Prices as usual.*
>
> *Box plan at Mr Angels, 11 High Street.*

In December of the following year, 1870, again for the Bedford Circus theatre, there appeared an advert, also in the *Devon Weekly Times*, for the next pantomime. Again, it is perhaps worthy of quoting:

55. Saxon Davis playing Mother Goose in 1932. Saxon was a fine comedienne and one of the country's leading pantomime dames, although today it is more traditional to have males playing the dame part.

Theatre Royal, Exeter.

Under new management of Mr Frederick Neebe.

*Tomorrow (Christmas Eve) will be produced the Grand Comic
Pantomime of Harlequin Blue Beard, or the King of the Cyclops
and the Girls of The Period.*

*Morning performances Monday December 28th and
Friday December 30th at two pm.*

*Special trains to Exmouth and Crediton on Wednesday December 28th
and to Newton and intermediate stations on Friday, 28th.*

Box plan at Mr Angels, 11 High Street.

The year 1889 saw the first pantomime at the rebuilt Theatre Royal in Longbrook Street. The pantomime, *Jack and the Beanstalk*, was sub-titled *"Harlequin
Little Bo-Peep. A Tale of Sheep, The Butcher Rude, The Fairy Goode and the Demons of
the Enchanted Wood"*. Ten years later, in December 1899, *The Daily Western Times*
review of *Cinderella* noted that "opening night indicates that it will rank amongst
the greatest of the successes which have given this house it pantomime renown."
The feature was, apparently, "the arrival of the coach and horses which was to
convey Cinderella to the Ball. The coaches were brilliantly illuminated and
the scene is almost dazzling to the eyes".

A few years later, in 1915,
Trewmans Exeter Flying Post reviewed
the first Exeter pantomime of the
Great War, *Mother Goose*. Cissie
Thompson played Colin Goose, and
the paper stated "of her songs she
makes the patriotic 'Your King and
Country Need You' a swinging
number, and 'Are We Down-
hearted?' invariably produces an
emphatic denial from the audience".
Pantomime songs have always been
unusual, innovative and frequently
tongue-twisting. For example, in
Mother Goose of 1915 the audience
were asked to sing the words 'Place
your lips like a solar eclipse – stewed
prunes and prisms'. Also included in
that show were some of Mr Percy
Cahill's songs, one of which was

56. *Clarkson Rose, who
appeared on more than one
occasion as 'Dame' in
Exeter pantomime, later
produced his show* Twinkle
at the theatre.

entitled 'Pimples on Pork'. The intriguing refrain – which no doubt the
audience enjoyed singing – was as follows:

You can't get many pimples on a pound of pickled pork,

Whether it comes from China, Japan or Carolina.

You can go to Pimlico, Chicago or New York,

But you can't get many pimples on a pound of pickled pork.

The *Flying Post* also reported that in *Mother Goose* "references to the War are very few". That changed the following year when the 1915/1916 pantomime was *Babes in the Wood*, which the newspaper stated was "compounded of two tales; that of the Babes in the Wood, and that of Robin Hood". Here, more mention is made of the hostilities going on at the time. Cissie Thompson again appears as Principal Boy, this time as Robin Hood. Two of her songs were 'All the boys in khaki get the nice girls', and 'Keep the home fires burning'. Maid Marian (played, incidentally, by a lady with the wonderfully theatrical name of Gladys Archbutt!) sings *The Army for me*. The paper reports that Will Scarlet "makes a decided success of *When we've wound up the watch on the Rhine*'. Another character in that pantomime was Gillie Potter. Some readers will recall him on radio as *The Sage of Hogsnorton*. The *Flying Post* notes that "his powers as a resourceful comedian find admirable scope in the Dame's part, and his song 'A little of what you fancy does you good' was a popular number".

Pantomimes were often written for specific theatres, and in many cases the authors were local people. It is not uncommon for theatre managers to 'write'

57. Arthur English (right) playing Alderman Fitzwarren in Dick Whittington, *1959–60. He is pictured here with Terry Wilson who played Martha.*

their own scripts – with a little help from their friends! Scripts would more than likely be bought in and adapted to suit the particular theatre. It is tradition to ensure that local names, places, personalities and events are entwined into the story – to give that extra interest and humour. Similarly, the majority of the pantomime music, if not all, would have been written by the resident musical director. In Exeter that was certainly the case, for Edmund Gaeton was a most experienced and capable musical director and composer.

Many characters are introduced into a pantomime, but some are instantly known and traditional, appearing in shows all over the country. Widow Twanky, Buttons, Dandini, Wishee and Washee, The Brokers Men, Baron Stoneybroke – all names that will be in various pantomimes wherever they occur. Others can vary with the writer, but he or she will more than likely include a name or two that reflects some part, or person, of the locality.

The very mention of the word 'pantomime' conjures up traditional characters – Principal Boy, The Dame, Demon King and others. Tradition and custom are the keywords of pantomime, and in this world of make-believe, pantomime tradition dictates that the Principal Boy is always a girl and the Dame is always a man! No panto would be quite the same if this were not so. Principal Boy will be a young lady who is the thigh-slapping champion of the people. The Dame, usually a more middle-aged actor, padded out more than necessary in all the right places, thus giving the appearance of a robust lady of advancing years. The Dame always has a sarcastic answer ready at hand, but will also be the butt of many jokes. The Demon King frequently appears from within a cloud of smoke following a small 'explosion' on stage. He does his best to make the children of the audience a little frightened of him, and encourage them to shout whenever he appears. Hopefully his very appearance from the wings will be rewarded with hisses and boos! Usually (and again in line with custom, or tradition) the Demon King, or similar character, appears from the opposite side to that of the Fairy Queen. That is what pantomime is about!

Over the centuries, pantomime has seen many 'characters'. In the early days there were Dan Leno, Herbertt Campbell, Vesta Tilley, Harriet Vernon and the clown of all clowns, Joseph Grimaldi. Later we saw Douglas Byng, George Lacy and Binnie Hale. More recently there were Fred Emney, Arthur Askey, and Nervo and Knox, who, with Naughton and Gould, created 'The Crazy Gang'. In addition to the 'names' on stage, we must not forget that pantomime is also presented by 'names'. In the early part of the last century Julian Wylie staged over one hundred pantos, and although he is, perhaps, not too well remembered these days, he was to earlier pantomime what the likes of Tom Arnold, or Prince and Emile Littler have been more recently.

Animals can play a considerable part of pantomime stories; they can always be introduced into the plot somehow, much to the excitement of children. The goose in Mother Goose, the cat in Dick Whittington, the dog in Mother

Hubbard, all played by actors in larger-than-life costume. Whilst actors usually play the animal parts, there are occasions, of course, when real animals are used. This adds to the delight of the children, and to the consternation of stage managers! The old adage is true – animals and children on stage can be a nightmare. The most usual live animals to be used are the ponies (often white) that pull Cinderella's coach, but frequently the scriptwriter will find an excuse to include acts involving other animals. Dogs, chimps, birds – any animal that could be classed as 'good box-office appeal" may be used, but animals are certainly not without their problems, and every theatre stage manager will be able to relate more than one story of some fraught scene involving the antics of such creatures!

Yet not everyone is happy with live animals appearing on stage. A report in the *Express & Echo* of December 2nd 1952, concerned the presentation of a petition with some 3,500 signatures to the Theatre Royal manager, Cliff Gwilliam. It had been organised by the south-western branch of the Performing Animals Defence League, and objected at the use of animals in the theatre,

59. Licence granted by the Lord Chamberlain for Dick Whittington, *1946–7.*

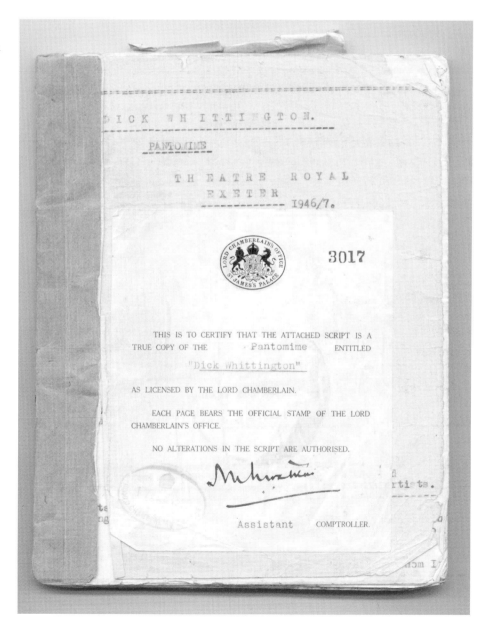

and similar petitions had been presented at other theatres throughout the country. Just why the petition was presented on that day remains a bit of a mystery, and even Cliff Gwilliam was reported to have been perplexed. The show at the Theatre Royal that week was the play *It's a Great Game*, based on a domestic situation in the north of England, and starred Leo Franklyn and Glenn Melvyn, but involved no animals. The forthcoming pantomime was to be *Aladdin*, but no animal acts had been booked for that production either.

Slapstick is also a traditional ingredient of panto. Two or more comedians will engage themselves in some knock-about routine, very often down stage of a cloth whilst a scene is being changed behind them. Although it may appear a 'rough and tumble', these are well-rehearsed acts, requiring stamina and a good sense of timing. Accidents seldom happen, but without constant rehearsal of their routines some of the participants could suffer serious injury. Time-honoured custard-pie throwing, wallpaper paste thrown 'accidentally' over someone, or water poured down the trousers of some poor stooge – all will raise great laughs and cheers from the audience. We all seem to enjoy seeing practical jokes played on others! Many comedians have spent a lifetime doing

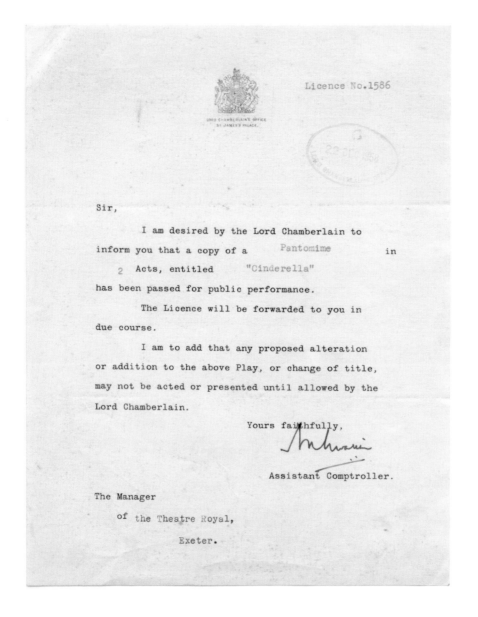

60. Notice of licence granted for Cinderella, *1958–9.*

such routines, and creating considerable impact with the public. The antics of Richard Hearne ('Mr Pastry'), Charlie Drake, Norman Wisdom and many others will long be remembered as the good, wholesome fun of the theatre. The stand-up act of Morecombe and Wise, frequently came close to slap-stick. At the Theatre Royal, Lauri Lupino Lane and George Truzzi were first seen in a slapstick routine when they were the robbers in the 1951/52 pantomime *Babes in the Wood*. In 1955/56, Tom, Dick and 'Arry, billed as the 'Continental Funsters', carried out similar routines. Wilbur & Franks were another slapstick act that appeared in Exeter for the 1947/48 show *Cinderella*. Other similar acts are still around, but few seem to echo the masters of slapstick that could be seen in pre- and post-war pantomime. Sadly, such comedians are fewer than they once were, possibly due to the demise of the music hall type of entertainment. It is a shame that so many comedians today seem to rely on a more coarse form of humour in their attempts to create laughter. No doubt they are popular with many of the younger public – but will they ever be taken to the hearts of an audience as were the likes of Max Wall, Norman Evans, Tommy Handley, Robb Wilton, Arthur Askey, or more recently Tommy Cooper?

61. Letter requesting lines to be omitted in the 1952 pantomime Aladdin.

LORD CHAMBERLAIN'S OFFICE,

ST JAMES'S PALACE, S.W 1.

19th December 1952

Dear Sir,

"Aladdin"

I am desired by the Lord Chamberlain to write to you regarding the additions to the above Pantomime, and to ask for an undertaking that in the Kitchen Scene, the lines from "I always take my little dog carpenter for a walk" down to "little jobs about the house" will be omitted.

The cheque for 5/- is returned herewith.

Yours faithfully,

Assistant Comptroller.

T.C.Gwilliam Esq.

Even 'Cheeky Chappie' Max Miller, who more often than not came very close to overstepping the mark, was well liked. He was frequently censored, and must have been closer to today's so-called alternative comedians than most of his era. Max was one of the few comedians of post-war entertainment who was frowned upon by many, but who would seem innocuous in today's more liberal society. He may have been the master of double entendre, but never resorted to obscenity itself. It was totally unacceptable then to swear or use obscenities on stage, or on radio. It proved, of course, that it was not a necessary part of the comedian's vocabulary.

It is interesting to compare modern comedy with the Lord Chamberlain's comments – or at least those of his Office – for a joke in the 1952 pantomime *Aladdin* at the Theatre Royal. It may seem difficult to believe now, some fifty years on, but the following banter between *Wishee* and *Washee* in the kitchen scene of that show received the famous 'blue pencil' through some lines of the script as they were considered unacceptable. To emphasise this, a letter was returned from that Office, with the script, requesting an undertaking that the following lines (duly highlighted in blue pencil) would be omitted:

Wishee: I always take my little dog Carpenter for a walk

Washee: Why do you call him Carpenter?

Wishee: He does little jobs about the house

Not exactly the bluest of jokes – but it does help to show the modern licence that entertainers enjoy today. Whether or not such freedom should be allowed is, of course, a personal issue.

In pantomime, transformation scenes can be one of the most attractive visual effects. The magic of one scene gently disappearing into something completely different is always well received by the audience. In the *Devon & Exeter Gazette* review of Percy Dunsford's *Cinderella* for 1936/37, the traditional transformation scene is highly acclaimed. 'The introduction to this spectacle of beauty and artistry is one of the most gorgeous front-cloth scenes ever originated at the Theatre Royal', it claims. It goes on to tell of a 'scene of dazzling splendour which gradually unfolded before the eyes of the astonished

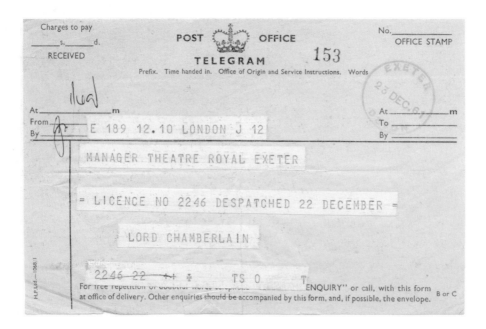

62. Telegram from the Lord Chamberlain advising that the licence for last pantomime, Ali Baba, had been despatched.

Cinderella'. In the following year, the *Express & Echo* claimed that in the pantomime *Mother Hubbard*, Percy Dunsford had 'once more given us one of those dazzling transformation scenes which only his actual genius…can render possible'.

There have surely been many, many people, both children and adults, who are left wondering how, for example, a village street can suddenly become a woodland scene. The method by which the magical 'transformation' is accomplished is really quite simple, and requires very little effort. It starts with a scene painted on a…but wait, perhaps that should be kept a secret. After all, if we *all* knew how it worked there would no longer be the surprise element; and pantomime should always be full of surprises!

The scenery for pantomime was large, bulky, and of considerable quantity. Yet at the Theatre Royal attention to detail was excellent. Perspective, shadow, colour – everything was done to produce the most magnificent sets. Backcloths were beautifully painted to produce anything from a baronial hall to a seaside picnic. The sheer size of each full cloth must have been daunting for the scenic artists. Not just one, but several were required for each pantomime. The ability

63. 'The Grand Coronation Pantomime' programme for Cinderella, *1936–7.*

of the artist to paint such splendid scenes on large canvas cloths, and at close quarters, was indeed professionalism. Such work was appreciated in the 1937/38 production Mother Hubbard, when the *Express & Echo* reported that 'the scene in which the snow ballet is staged probably surpasses anything previously attempted in Theatre Royal pantomimes'. It goes on to mention 'the dazzling white of the snow and frostbound trees, accentuated by the costumes of the dancers, and the twinkling of the innumerable lights on the trees and sleigh adding to the effect'.

The artists worked from sketches, and painted the cloths when they were stretched on a large frame. At the Theatre Royal, due to the limited size of the paint room, it was only possible to step back a few feet to check their work. It was not until the cloth was actually hung on stage that they were able to see the whole finished article. The perspective and detail was such that, when viewed from the auditorium, the finished product was proof of their amazing talents. So often a path across a field in the distance seemed to go out the back of the

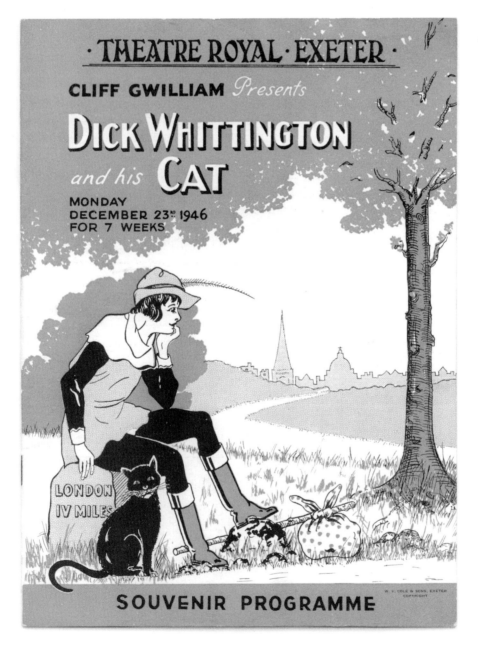

64. *Pantomime programme for* Dick Whittington, *1946–7 with Hilda Campbell Russell in the title role.*

theatre; or the staircase painted on a cloth would be linked in with an actual flight of stairs, giving the appearance of being almost never ending. In the *Devon and Exeter Gazette* of December 27th, 1924, the scenery for *Dick Whittington* is highly regarded. The Highgate Hill scene is claimed to be 'one of the most artistic scenes in the pantomime, designed and modelled by Mr Dunsford, and painted by Roland Browne, and is an artistic triumph'. Some thirty years later, Peter J. Jarman reviewed Cliff Gwilliam's production of that show, the *Express & Echo* reporter telling of scenes being 'splashed vividly with colour'.

Many incredible creations appeared on the stage at Longbrook Street, all the work of a handful of people, but notably for many years by scene painter Roland Browne, mentioned above. His ability, and that of his successors, including Nicholas Jean and William Stewart, provided some incredible scenes on the flats and cloths. In the Theatre's latter years the scenic artist was another highly respected painter – George Sinclair, who possessed a similar talent. It seems a pity to realise that after a show has finished its run, many cloths and sets would either be sold, or repainted as a different scene and used in another show. So many painstaking hours had gone into the work, only to be obliterated forever. The scene painters of today's theatre no doubt have the same professional ability, but probably work in far better surroundings and with much improved materials.

As mentioned earlier, it was, and still is, necessary to attract 'names' to appear in pantomimes to make it profitable. During the early part of the twentieth century some of the stars appearing at Exeter were Percy Cahill (in 1914 and 1921), Gillie Potter, who played Abanazaar in the 1919 show *Aladdin*, and Saxon Davis. Saxon Davis had become a national figure by the time she made her third appearance at Exeter, as Mother Goose in 1932 (with Hay Plumb as King Gander). She was Mrs Sinbad in 1933/34, and an ugly sister in *Cinderella* during the coronation year production of 1936/37, when the comedienne made her

65. War time air raid warning, advising patrons that cover could be taken under the 'steel and concrete' circle if required.

sixth appearance at the Theatre Royal. Hay Plumb was a noted comedian and appeared in the 1929/30 production of *Babes in the Wood*, when the *Devon & Exeter Gazette* referred to him as 'old old and tried friend, as entertaining as ever'. The paper states that he 'gives a delicious presentation, full of his usual rich vintage of humour'.

Albert Grant was another much admired comedian, who appeared in Exeter for the first time in 1935/36, in *Dick Whittington*, and two years later was in *Mother Hubbard*, followed by *Mother Goose* in 1938/39, appearing in both of those shows with Hay Plumb. In reviewing Mother Hubbard, the *Express & Echo* greeted Albert Grant 'with delight', and continued 'he is a comedian with individuality'. Following Percy Dunsford's death in 1940, Albert H. Grant was invited to produce the pantomime at Exeter for that year. So many actors and actresses have appeared in pantomime at the Theatre Royal that, as before, it would be unrealistic to mention them all within these pages. More recently, and since the end of the last War, several names appeared more than once in

66. Pantomime programme for the theatre's Diamond Jubilee production of Mother Goose, *1948—9.*

58

an Exeter pantomime. Those readers who perhaps saw the shows year after year will recall many of them.

Albert Whelan appeared in variety shows in the city, and was at the Theatre Royal as Quang Ho! in the 1948/49 production of *Mother Goose*. He took the part of Man Friday in *Robinson Crusoe* the following year.

Hilda Campbell Russell was Principal Boy at Exeter's pantomimes on several occasions, and one of the top Principal Boys of her era. As early as 1946 she starred in Exeter as Dick Whittington, and was Prince Charming in *Cinderella* the following year. Hilda appeared as Robin Hood in 1951 and was at the Theatre again in 1957/58 when she played Robinson Crusoe. A popular and talented actress, she appeared at theatres across the country. Hilda Campbell Russell died in 2002 aged over ninety, but shortly before her death she fondly recalled her stage career, and claimed in an interview that if the right part were available she would take it!

Holt and Maurice, a comedy duo, played the Ugly Sisters in *Cinderella* of

67. Pantomime programme for Robinson Crusoe, *1949–50.*

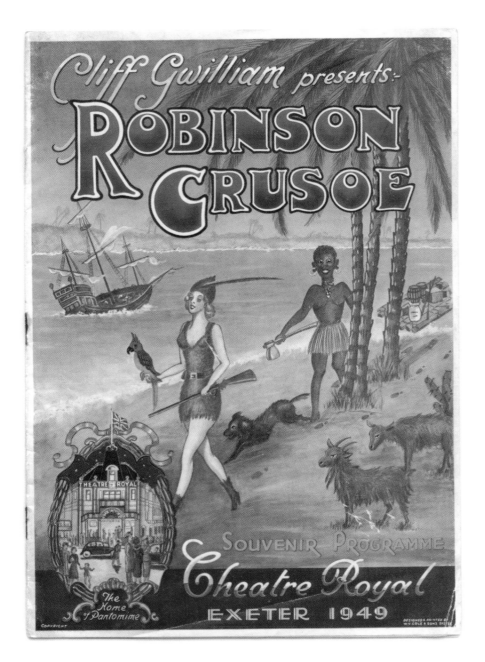

1947/48 and in 1948/49 Louis Holt was Mother Goose, with Bert Maurice as King Krakpot. They also made frequent appearances in variety revues.

Stella Holles was another popular visitor to Exeter, her Dandini in the 1947/48 show *Cinderella* was well received, and she was invited back the following year to play Princess Penelope, the principal girl in the production of *Robinson Crusoe*.

Randolph Sutton appeared as Will Scarlett in the 1951/52 panto *Babes in the Wood*. Well known as a 'personality', Randolph Sutton had been in the theatre world for many years. He appeared in the *Babes* production with the equally well known George Truzzi and Lupino Lane.

George Truzzi and Lauri Lupino Lane made an appearance as the robbers in 1951/52, and the following year were Wishee and Washee in *Aladdin*, when Mary Meredith played the lead part. George Truzzi's wife had a miniature circus that also appeared here, her speciality act being performing poodles! Lauri Lupino Lane came from a famous theatrical family. Members of the

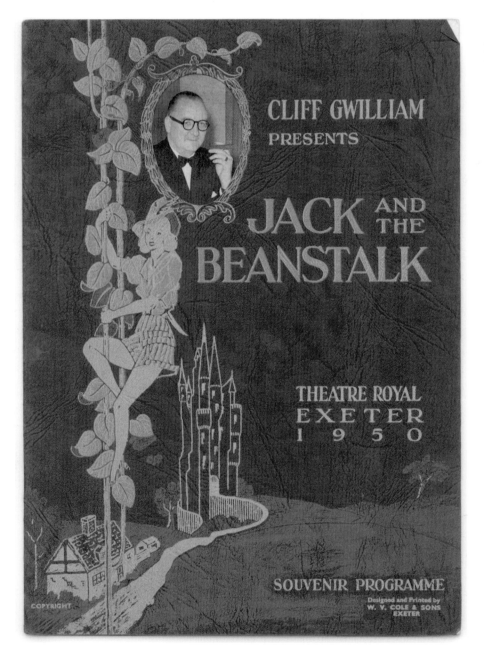

68. *Pantomime programme for* Jack and the Beanstalk, *1950–1.*

*69. Order of Service for
pantomime Sunday,
January 1950.*

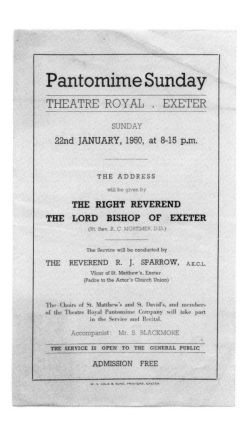

Lupino family had, at various times, played most theatres in the British Isles over a period of many years.

Clarkson Rose appeared here on more than one occasion as pantomime dame. He was also responsible for bringing his show *Twinkle* to Exeter in 1962 for its first resident season in the City, which unfortunately turned out to be the last time the show was to visit Exeter. *Twinkle* was a variety show created by Clarkson Rose and Olive Fox. Its content was standard 'variety show' acts – comedians, singers, dancers, sketches and so on. In the final souvenir programme, Norman Wisdom claimed that *Twinkle* was the show with 'the lot'. For many artistes, it was such shows that helped to start them on a life in the theatre. Some even started with that company as back-stage assistants before venturing onto the stage itself. Clarkson Rose had been a respected theatrical name in this country's theatre world for many years, but it is sad to know that instead of finishing his days in comfort and with dignity, he was the victim of a massive embezzlement by an employee and died almost penniless.

During the 1957 *Robinson Crusoe*, when Clarkson Rose was Dame Crusoe, Exeter had a glimpse of another personality in the making. Appearing in that production was a very popular singing group known as "The Four Ramblers" – and one of the four was a young man by the name of Val Doonican. Few people can say they do not know *that* name!

In 1959 a famous comedian appeared as Alderman Fitzwarren in *Dick Whittington*. He was Arthur English, the cockney 'spiv' with the outrageous suits and ties. Remember his catch phrase 'open the cage, start the music' ? In more recent years he often appeared on television.

Johnny Dallas was another visitor in the fifties, playing such parts as Buttons and Jimmy Goose. He also played Dame Cassim Baba in the last pantomime at the Royal – *Ali Baba* – when Tony "Silly Thing" Scott and Lola MacDonald also appeared.

For the record, *Ali Baba* had not been seen in Exeter for forty years, when it had been known as *Forty Thieves*. Advertisements in the 1920 programme of that show offered Old Tawny Port from the Devon & Somerset Stores at six shillings a bottle (the cost today would be at least £3 a bottle!); Cornish's were selling a gentleman's raincoat for only 35 shillings (£1.75p); and it was possible to buy a sports coat from Jas. Pulsford, High Street, for just 19/11d, or £1 today! Few advertisements in the 1961 programme displayed prices, but it would have been possible to have a three course evening dinner at the Greyhound Hotel in Sidwell Street for just 12/6d (62p) per head. Sadly, or perhaps in a way luckily, the audiences for the run of *Ali Baba* were not to know that they would never be able to see another pantomime at the Theatre Royal, for later the next year the theatre was to close its doors to the public for the last time.

Most pantomimes had special attractions. Many were unbelievably spectacular for those days, and notably so was Jimmie Curries Waterfall. This first appeared at Exeter in 1953, and again in 1960/61. During a pantomime,

70. *Pantomime programme for* Babes in the Wood, *1951–2*

over a million of gallons of water would cascade in front of the audience – usually in the first half of the show to allow the stage crew to mop up the stage during the interval!

Kirby's Flying Ballet always produced many exciting moments for the audience, and appeared in Exeter as early as the 1931 production of *Goody Two Shoes* and again in 1948/49 during the Theatre's diamond jubilee production of *Mother Goose*. In 1952/53, *Aladdin* presented The Policeman's Flying Ballet for the first time in the West Country, and that show also had Eugene's Flying ballet – directed by Arthur Kirby. Those involved would be suspended on a thin but very strong piano wire attached to a harness. Characters would 'fly' across, up, and down the stage. One wonders what the insurance premium would have been!

Many other 'specialities' were engaged to add something special to the pantomime season. Vincent Tildsley's Master Singers in 1948/49, The Dagenham Girl Pipers in 1953/54, Madame Truzzi's Miniature Circus of ponies and dogs in 1954/55, and many others. In today's theatre there may be more,

71. Pantomime programme for the Coronation Year, 1952–3 for the production of Aladdin.

72. A typical page from 'Uncle Percy's Pantomime Album', shown here for the 1938–9 show Mother Goose. *Several addresses are from various locations in Devon and Somerset showing the popularity of Exeter's pantomimes. Eight-year old Roy Coombs could not then have been aware that he would eventually become stage manager for Exeter Amateur Operatic Society!*

and doubtless better, spectacles involving computerized operations and laser effects. Over fifty years ago there was neither the technology nor cash available to stage some of the huge extravaganzas witnessed today. Even so, what was seen then was as dramatic as it could possibly have been for the period.

Local personalities have sometimes appeared in the Theatre Royal pantomimes. Some were in their own right, such as Ruth Stabb and Angela Casalucci, and others as a group. Ruth was a well-known dance teacher in Exeter. She appeared with Joan Booth in the 1954/55 production of *Cinderella*, and arranged the ballet and dances for *Jack & The Beanstalk* the following year. In the 1956/57 pantomime *Mother Goose*, Ruth played Fairy Fortuna. Angela appeared with Dorothy Sutton as 'the babes' in the 1951/52 production of *Babes in the Wood*.

Probably the most well known local group to take part in Theatre Royal pantomimes was Olga Cooper's Young Ladies. Olga Cooper formed 'The Exeter Ballet' for the wartime production of Dick Whittington in 1941. Amongst the local young ladies making up that group were Patricia Davis, Stella Glynn, Pamela Prince, Joy Lowe, Barbara Pearce and Audrey Pidgeon. It also included Ruth Stabb, mentioned above, and Babs Westcott who, like Ruth, was also to make her mark on dance tuition in the city. Olga Cooper's talented dance troupes brought a taste of theatre to many local girls, and they acted as back-up dance troupe for numerous pantos. It was customary for a professional dance troupe to take the main billing, and a second troupe, frequently local, to act as back-up. Her 'Dancing Twelve' appeared in the 1946 Production of *Dick Whittington*.

In 1947 the Phyllis Scanes Young Ladies troupe appeared, under the auspices of the person who probably taught half of Exeter to dance. In 1948, Olga

Cooper's Young Ladies returned, and seem to have been a permanent fixture until what would appear to be their last appearance in 1957 – although in that year they were billed as the 'Olga Cooper Young Ladies of the Ballet'. Olga Cooper was a highly talented dance teacher, well known throughout the country for her expertise. Not only did she teach dance, she was also requested to act as choreographer for many shows all over the South West. Later in her career she was much in demand as a dance examiner, and on many occasions was flown to other countries to act in that capacity.

Professional dance companies appeared at virtually every Theatre Royal pantomime in the twentieth century. Madame Walker's Acadamy Girls were probably the most frequent visitors to Exeter, with The Marie De Vere Dance Troupe and Larry Gordon's Dance Troupe being other national names in the dance world that regularly appeared at the Theatre. During those post-war pantomime runs countless local young ladies spent their evenings dancing around the Theatre Royal stage. It would be interesting to know how many went on to dance professionally. Certainly one did, for a young Sally Dawson, who had danced many times on stage in Exeter, joined the Bluebell Girls at the Paris Lido.

Every pantomime has memories for those in the audience. The already mentioned 'spectacles' will, of course, remain uppermost for many, but others will recall other parts of the shows. Finales at one time were quite spectacular, with a big musical number to give the ending a flourish, not just the cast walking on stage to take a bow. Even war did not seem to dampen the pantomime spirit, for at the start of the 1939/40 pantomime *Aladdin*, Percy Dunsford proudly proclaimed that he intended "going on with this pantomime just as if Hitler had never been on the map of Europe"! Indeed, *Aladdin* contained musical numbers that referred directly to the War that had recently been declared. *Wish me luck as you wave me goodbye* and *There'll always be an England* were just two of the patriotic songs. The *Express & Echo* review of the first of the wartime pantomimes noted 'The shadow of war, blackout regulations and transport restrictions are some of the adverse conditions under which the 51st panto has been prepared. It is the English nature to triumph over difficulties and to transmute them into solaces. Topics of the moment, from darkened

73. Olga Cooper's 'Young Ladies' dance group. Olga was one of Exeter's leading dance teachers, and her pupils frequently appeared at Exeter pantomimes.

streets to ration books, have produced ideas that are the perfect antidote to the cares of everyday life'.

Throughout the war, the Theatre Royal continued to stage productions, including pantomime, albeit with some difficulty at times. The musical director, Edmund Gaeton, was temporarily replaced during the war years as he was on war service. One of his replacements was the aptly named Alfred C. Toone! A Chinese group of acrobats, Four Yuk Ching, was unable to appear in the 1939 pantomime as the Home Office refused clearance for their plane to land in this country. Miss Pearce, the wardrobe mistress, was faced with the problem of finding suitable material to make the often exotic costumes. The 1940/41 pantomime had no mention of the war in its reviews, but the following year, *Dick Whittington*, was reported by the *Express & Echo* as 'a complete triumph over wartime difficulties', and a similar notice appeared for the 1944 production of *Jack & The Beanstalk*. The 1945/46 pantomime *Babes in the Wood* was simply reported as being 'the victory panto', and it was of course Cliff Gwilliam's first as manager.

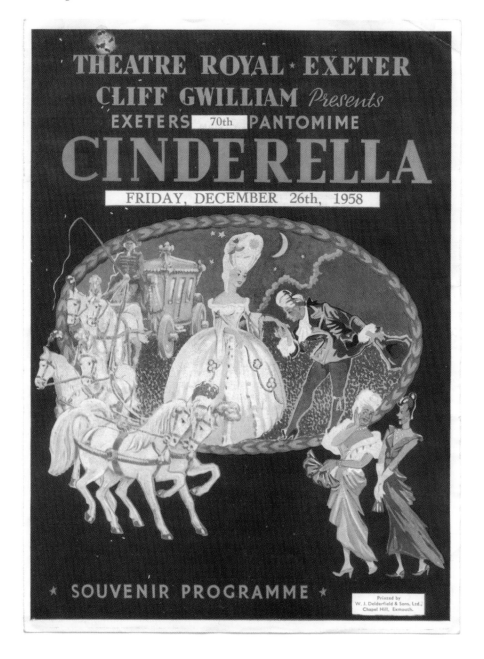

74. *Programme for the 70th Pantomime* Cinderella, *1958–9.*

Children will usually remember the Demon King, or King Rat because they were the 'baddies'. They will also remember the song-sheets, when a large cloth was lowered on stage, usually at the front whilst a scene change took place behind. On the cloth were the words of a song, and children in the stalls were encouraged to sing louder than the children in the circle, or vice-versa. No matter who won, each night there would be a very happy number of children shouting out the words on the song-sheet.

Pantomime held something for all ages. Grandparents and parents would take children, who eventually would grow up to do the same. It was a time of that magical something which we all can associate with theatre, a time of enjoyment, laughter and happiness. Yet pantomime also had its serious times. Shortly after the annual pantomime started its run, it was traditional for staff of the Theatre Royal to join the pantomime company and members of the public for a religious service on stage. Held on a Sunday evening, with admission free of course, it became a popular and well-attended event. For many years the Reverend Sparrow, Vicar of St Matthews Church and padre to the Exeter

75. Programme for the last ever Pantomime at the theatre – Ali Baba, 1961–2.

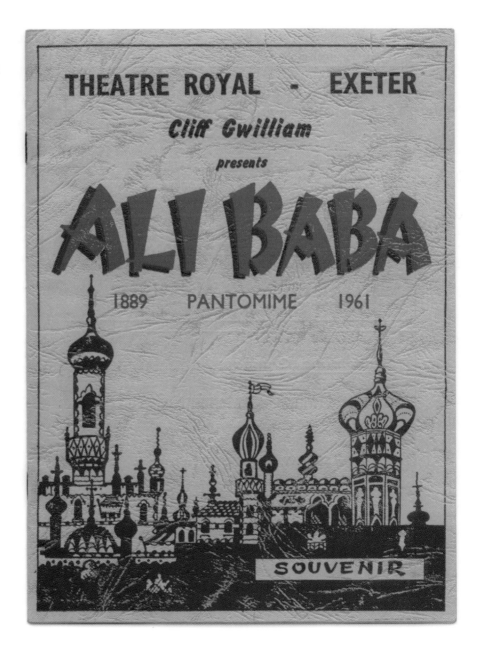

THEATRE ROYAL - EXETER

Cliff Gwilliam

presents

ALI BABA

1889   PANTOMIME   1961

SOUVENIR

branch of the Actors Church Union, led the service, accompanied by the choirs of the local churches of St Matthew and St David, plus the theatre orchestra. In earlier days there was another Service held at the Theatre on Good Fridays, but this seems to have disappeared for some reason.

Another custom was that at some point towards the end of the pantomime run, representatives of the cast would be invited to meet the Mayor at Guildhall. A means of the Mayor expressing thanks on behalf of the city to the cast and production team, this annual gathering was looked upon as an important part of the pantomime season. When the theatre opened after the fire of 1887, the directors had a "medal" struck in silver, and each year it was presented to the incoming Mayor at Guildhall. It became a tradition that on Civic night, when the Mayor and members of the city council attended the pantomime the medal would be used, allowing free entry to the theatre. At the same time, special programmes were presented to the civic party. These were printed on silk, with a decorative edging, and these remained a tradition until just a few years before the theatre closed. Some years before the last war, the medal was lost, and it was not until 1944 that it re-appeared. Rowland Glave Saunders had been Mayor for most of the Second World War, and a former chairman of the Exeter Theatre Company, and towards the end of his mayoralty he discovered the medal in a desk drawer at the Mayor's parlour at Guildhall. Having completed his last term in office, he held a small ceremony at Guildhall, where he presented the medal to the incoming Mayor, Ald. Vincent Thompson. Unfortunately it disappeared once again, and to date has never been found.

76. *Adverts for some of the companies that supplied coaches to bring patrons from outlying areas to the theatre.*

Transport To The Show

Such was the drawing power of pantomime in Exeter that special transport arrangements were made for patrons to get to and from the theatre. Despite the fact that the Theatre Royal was in the centre of the city, and it is doubtful that any future theatre could get closer to the centre than the Royal, it was still thought necessary to provide special buses and trains.

In the latter days of the theatre the motorcar was beginning to appear in greater numbers, although even in the fifties it was not an accepted part of the family inventory as it is today. Earlier years, however, saw the motorcar as a rarity, and an item only for those in our society who could have afforded such a luxury. For the remainder, getting about demanded the use of public transport, or simply walking.

Those living within the city had a regular bus route operating in most areas. It should be borne in mind that in those days Alphington, Ide, Pinhoe and Topsham were then county villages, and not city suburbs. For the inhabitants of those and other villages there was not a regular bus service of the same frequency as was enjoyed in the City. Some villages may have had just a few buses each week. For patrons in rural areas it was the train; and in those days, of course, trains stopped at every little halt and village. For example, in 1934 the Pantomime Special train from Bovey Tracey to St David's Station would stop at no less than eleven stations – over a distance of just a few miles by rail. The cost of a third class return ticket from Bovey was then 1/6d.or 7½ pence today!

Old handbills issued by the Great Western Railway listed the names of the various stopping places in the Exeter area. These places, long since passed by way of the 'Beeching axe' and other regrettable cut-backs, included Cove Halt, Burlescombe, Yeo Mill Halt, Burn, Brimley Halt, Ide Halt,

77. Great Western Railway timetable and prices for special trains to Mother Hubbard, *1937–8. The maximum price shown (3s. 2d.) would today be about 15 pence!*

78. Before the Second World War there were several specific car parks in the locality of the theatre. Some of these disappeared during the blitz on Exeter in 1942.

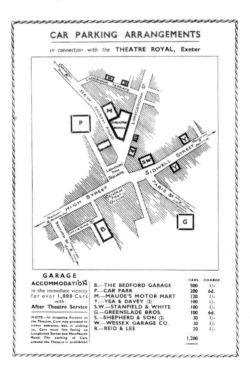

79. Silk programme for
Cinderella, *1909. These
programmes were specially
made and given to the
Civic party on Mayoral
Night each year. This
practice continued almost
until the theatre closed.*

Brampford Speke. These are names that could almost earn their place in a Betjeman poem!

Special trains were met at St David's Station by special buses to and from the Theatre. The 'bus stop outside the Jolly Porter Inn at St David's had a destination plate on a pole, and the destinations included "Theatre", taking potential patrons virtually to the Theatre doors. Even though the Theatre Royal ceased to exist in 1962, this plate continued to display "Theatre" until 1969, thus causing theatre-goers a problem, because that service went to the City centre, and nowhere near the Northcott Theatre which opened in 1967! Whilst this form of transport added to the cost of the evening out, it was a service that served the Theatre well – and encouraged vast numbers in outlying areas to visit the Exeter pantomime. In the early part of the last century there were many who seldom left their village or town, and thus an 'outing' to the pantomime in Exeter was an annual event, to be talked about for weeks afterwards.

Others came by what was then known as a 'charabanc', or coach. Some villages would be able to fill more than one coach. The coach party remains, of course, an accepted method of getting to entertainment in the City for those who have no other means, or who do not wish to use their own transport. Coaches can regularly be seen arriving for shows, concerts and festivals at various venues in the City. Taylor's Central Garages, Greenslades' Tours, Royal Blue Express, Devon General Omnibus & Touring Company, and Grey Cars were just some of the coach operators serving the Theatre Royal.

80. In 1890 the theatre's pantomime was Jack & The Beanstalk. *Here, an early poster for that show advertises "morning" performances at 2 pm, on Tuesdays and Fridays. These performances tended to be popular and increased the traffic bringing patrons to the theatre.*

In post-war days of the late forties and fifties, if the Theatre Royal was reached by car, then there were several car parks drivers were recommended to use. In the Theatre Royal era, the programmes stipulated that parking in the immediate vicinity of the Theatre was prohibited, although this was way before the days of 'yellow lines'. Apart from on-street parking some distance away, certain car parks were made available for the use of patrons, and there were always maps in the Theatre programmes indicating the various parks available

In the adjacent 'official' car parking areas, over one thousand cars could be accommodated, at a charge of either one shilling or sixpence – or in today's equivalent, 5 pence or 2 ½ pence! During those years, however, few people had their own cars, and as the Theatre seating capacity was in the region of one thousand, it is very doubtful that all of those spaces were used on any one night. Today, we are often desperate for places to park.

Over the years, every one of the designated areas shown on the programme map has disappeared. The last to vanish was the car park behind what was the Savoy (later the ABC) cinema in Northernhay Place. This was capable of holding in the region of 200 cars, but disappeared in the mid sixties, and is now an office block. Even the cinema itself has now been demolished.

It is slightly strange to note that, according to the instructions in the programmes, drivers could drop their passengers at either theatre entrance, but on collection after the show, vehicles were instructed to line facing *up* Longbrook Street and New North Road! It must be assumed that this was in order to have all the waiting vehicles on one side.

Pantomime Scenes

81. *A typical 'frontcloth' scene being acted out during a scene change, here in* Babes in the Wood, 1960/61. *Note the trip wire indicating the edge of the stage above the orchestra pit. In earlier years there were footlights across the front of the stage.*

82. *It was traditional for the theatre manager, Cliff Gwilliam, to make a speech on the last night of pantomimes. All of the principal artistes would receive small gifts, and these can be seen on the stage floor at the end of* Mother Goose *in 1956/57.*

83. *Pickles (Stan Van), Dame Trott (Charlie Ellis) and The Squire (Horace Mashford) in a scene from* Jack & the Beanstalk, 1955/56. *Leon and Kiki played Jenny the Cow!*

84. One of the ballroom scenes during Cinderella, *1958/59. Margaret Freer played the lead role, with Johnny Dallas playing Buttons.*

85. Cinderella (Carole Keith) tries on the slipper, assisted by Buttons (Louis Roberts). The 1954/55 production of Cinderella *included genuine twins – The Burt Twins – as the Ugly Sisters, seen on the right of the picture.*

86. The finale of Mother Goose *1956/57. Centre stage are Jeanette Landis, as Colin Goose, and Charlie Ellis as Mother Goose. Fairy Fortuna, on the extreme left, was played by local dancer Ruth Stabb.*

87. Robinson Crusoe *in 1957/58, included 'The Four Ramblers', a male quartet. Seen here in the parts of four fishermen, the gentleman in front of the Topsham lifebelt is none other than Val Doonican. Dame Crusoe, centre, was played by Clarkson Rose.*

88. *'The Valley of Diamonds' – a dramatic scene from Percy Dunsford's production of* Sinbad the Sailor *in 1933/34. Sinbad was played by Enid Lowe, with Saxon Davis playing his mother. During the first week of the show there were 2pm matinees every day. The production was reported as being 'rich in mirth, music and dance'.*

89. *A scene from the 1950/51 production of* Jack & The Beanstalk. *Betty Lotinga played Jack, with Max Brewster as Dame.*

90. *Prince Charming (Linda Hagan) takes the hand of Cinderella (Margaret Freer), watched by Dandini (Estelle Russell) and The Fairy (Jill Alison), 1958/59.*

91. *Cinderella's gilded coach, pulled by two white ponies, in the 1954/55 production. Pamela De Waal played The Fairy.*

92. *The opening scene from* Red Riding Hood, *1909/10. Although this show had previously been seen in 1893, it was not staged at the theatre after 1910.*

93. *Dick Whittington (Marion Gordon) shares a tense moment with Alice Fitzwarren (Pat Whelan). Watching over them is The Fairy (Pamela De Waal) 1954/55.*

94. *The Four Gibson Girls appeared in the 1958/59 production of* Cinderella.

95. Ali Baba *in 1961/62 was the last pantomime at the theatre. The Caliph (Edward J. Wood) sits centre stage to watch his exotic dancers.*

*96. One of the splendid
backcloths devised by scenic
artists at Exeter. Many were
painted in the scenic
artists' studio backstage.
The cloths, the full height
and width of the stage, were
incredibly detailed.*

*97. A fairground scene
from* Dick Whittington,
1959/60.

98. The finale of Dick
Whittington *in 1959/60.*

99. *A scene from the 1940/41 production of* Jack & The Beanstalk. *Pantomimes continued throughout the war. The theatre was fortunate in that it never received a direct hit in the bombing raids on Exeter, although there was superficial damage as a result of nearby buildings being destroyed.*

100. *Together at last! Alice Fitzwarren and Dick Whittington share a tender moment in 1951/52.*

101. *The magic hour arrives in the 1958/59 production of* Cinderella! *Linda Hagan (Prince Charming) and Margaret Freer (Cinderella) share centre stage during the ball, as midnight starts to chime.*

102. During Babes in the Wood, *children in the audience were enthralled by Miss Barbara's chimpanzees and 'educated Alsatian dog', 1960/61. In this picture, some of the cast get to know the chimps. Live animals always proved popular to pantomime audiences, though not always with the stagehands.*

103. Jimmie Currie's Famous Waterfall Spectacle used over one million gallons of water during Dick Whittington, *1953/54. That show included The Dagenham Girl Pipers, seen here in the waterfall scene with other members of the cast.*

104. Local dancers The Olga Cooper Young Ladies joined forces with Don Ross's Famous Young Ladies in the 1950/51 production of Jack & The Beanstalk. *The action shown is during a scene from that show, the Transformation to Fairyland.*

105. Jack (Betty Lotinga) protects his friends during a battle with The Giant in the kitchen scene from Jack & The Beanstalk, *1950/51.*

106. Four ponies pulled the dazzling coach in the 1936 production of Cinderella. *Janet Morrison, in the title role, is assisted from her coach by Buttons (Guy North) as she arrives at The Ball in a scene from that show. The show was billed as "The Grand Coronation Pantomime".*

107. The amazing detail seen in Alderman Fitzwarren's stores for the 1935/36 production of Dick Whittington. *Even though there are no actors on stage, the scene still manages to look 'busy'.*

108. A baronial hall scene in one of George Sinclair's superb backcloths. Perspective and shadow give the impression of a huge room. George was the last scenic artist employed at the theatre.

109. A scene from Babes in the Wood, *1960/61. The bridge takes us away from the stage, whilst a castle on the hill gives tremendous height to the scene. Such backcloths add a great deal of interest to any pantomime scene.*

Amateur Productions

The Theatre was the venue not only of professional shows and pantomimes, but also a considerable number by amateur groups. One of Devon's 'characters' was A. J. (Bert) Coles, probably better known as Jan Stewer, whose mastery of the Devon dialect was unequalled. At the Theatre Royal in July 1911, his show *Revel Day* was billed as 'a real Devonshire musical comedy'. The show was written by Coles, and performed by the Jan Stewer Amateur Operatic Company of 'nearly 50 artistes'. During the show, opera glasses could be obtained from an attendant for sixpence (5 pence), Fry's chocolates could be purchased in boxes from one penny to half a crown, and freshly made coffee was just two pence a cup. One penny is almost impossible to equate today, but half a crown would be fifteen pence!

110. The 1958 production of Exeter Amateur Operatic Society's New Moon. *This society staged their shows at the theatre until it closed. Several of the cast in the photograph are still society members.*

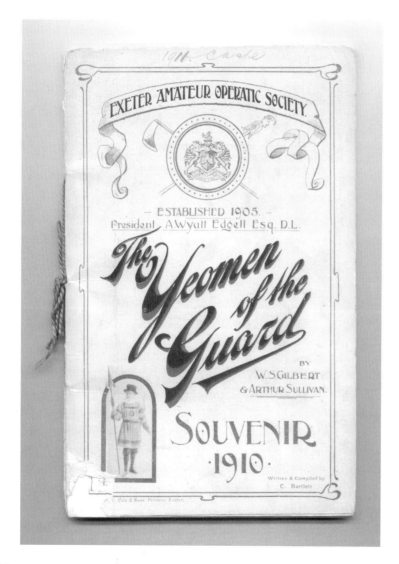

111. In 1910, Yeoman of the Guard *was the Exeter Amateur Operatic Society's sixth performance. In those days the programmes were most elaborate. The one shown opposite contained over fifty pages, eight of which were a summary of the show. There were no less than sixty small photographs, mainly of the cast – apart from those in the many advertisements. Quite a document!*

112. When the Exeter University staged Princess Ida *in 1962, it was one of the last amateur companies to perform on that stage. It was a new production, specially devised by producer Christine Caldwell. Their programme, shown above, was designed on the lines of a Civic Night silk programme.*

On Wednesday, April 24th, 1912 the Exeter Amateur Players staged Wilde's *The Importance of Being Earnest* in aid of the Exeter City Supporters' Football Club. In the show, Mr Worthing's butler was played by Paul Tighe, later to become a director of the Theatre Royal.

Probably one of the most regular of amateur events was the annual show produced by the Exeter Amateur Operatic Society. This Society probably performed at the Theatre on more occasions than any other local amateur company. For several decades the Society took over the theatre for a week, and originally staged light opera, but later added many musicals to its repertoire. There are still several people living locally who can claim to have been members of the Society before the last war, and since then many local people have also been involved with the Exeter Amateur Operatic Society. Until 1962, most of these members would have had the pleasure of appearing on stage at the

113. *The Exeter Schools'
music festival gave children
the opportunity to perform
on a professional stage. The
children shown here were
Ladysmith School pupils of
Mrs Griffiths' class in
1951, performing their act
entitled 'Lanterns and
Fans'.*

Theatre Royal. The programme for *Merrie England* in 1946, their first production
after the end of hostilities, contains many well-known names in the City's
amateur theatre world of that era – James Whiteside, Harold Gayton, Leonard
Searle Smale, Walter Daw, Leonard & Edythe Crump, Gordon Kerslake, Stanley
Whitburn, Clarion Bahr, Gwendoline Spray and many others whose
contribution to the amateur stage continued for many years.

There was always a completely amateur cast. Nevertheless it frequently played
to capacity audiences, and it was always highly satisfactory for the officers of
the Society proudly to place the 'House Full' sign at the Theatre entrance.
Bearing in mind the Theatre capacity was in excess of 900, to fill it for an
amateur show was no mean feat. To do so for most evenings of the week was
incredible. This would be difficult to achieve these days, but of course
Exeter has no theatre capable of seating so many. Even this company
experienced difficulty in attracting their audiences, however, and it was
reported in the press that whilst in 1953 (*Merrie England*) the Exeter
Amateur Operatic Society played to 5,321 paying customers during
their week's run, in 1954 (*Rebel Maid*) that figure had dropped to
only 3,414. Perhaps *Rebel Maid* was not as popular as *Merrie England*, but
the difference of almost two thousand patrons that year must
had made a considerable financial problem. Following the closure of
the Theatre Royal, the company

114. *The Exeter Amateur
Players were one of several
local groups that staged
plays at the theatre. In* The
Importance of Being
Earnest *in 1912, Mr Paul
Tighe played the part of the
butler, Merriman. Tighe
was a chemist in the city
and later became a director
of the Exeter Theatre
Company.*

staged their 1963 and 1964 shows at St Georges Hall (where many Society members will recall the unfortunate but distinctive odour of fish and rotten fruit sometimes drifting on stage during the show!), and in 1965 they moved to the former Savoy Cinema, where they also played to full houses, until the opening of the Northcott Theatre.

Many other shows by amateur groups were presented at the Theatre. The University College of the South West (now Exeter University) had music and drama societies, and both performed at the Theatre. In March1962 the University staged a special production of Gilbert and Sullivan's *Princess Ida*. It was devised and produced by Christine Caldwell to mark the centenary of the founding of the Royal Albert Memorial College, and it is from this that the University's student body has since been known as the "RAMS", taking a ram's head as its crest.

The Devon Players staged a large number of productions there, even as far back as 1929, although not necessarily each year. Their efforts were frequently rewarded with large audiences and excellent reviews. Their production of *An Inspector Calls* in 1952 was, according to Peter Jarman, drama critic of the *Express & Echo*, 'a shining example of endeavour and integrity. If all amateurs were like Devon Players what an achievement that would be'.

Over a period of several years, hundreds of youngsters appeared on the Theatre's stage in the Exeter and District Schools Music Association annual festivals. What a wonderful experience that must have been for countless schoolchildren of Exeter – to be appearing on the stage of their 'own' Theatre! The festivals were always well received – even if they had somewhat captive audiences! Mums and Dads would obviously want to see their off-springs 'on stage', and no doubt the audiences were swelled by grans and granddads, uncles

115. Merrie England *was the first post war show for the Exeter Amateur Operatic Society, 1946. Their president, Roland Glave Saunders, had been mayor during most of the war years.*

and aunts and whoever else could be persuaded to go along. Various local schools presented acts of singing, dancing, recitals etc., and no doubt for some of these young people such appearances were perhaps the 'taster' for later involvement in amateur productions, or possibly the start of a professional career.

Local dancing schools would hold their annual 'showcase' event there, and on Sundays there would sometimes be concerts by local bands and orchestras. Devon Opera also staged shows at the Royal, and in 1951 presented *Il Trovatore* – their first major production. Following that success, in 1952 they presented *Carmen*, not the easiest of operas for an amateur company to stage. In many of their performances some principals were brought in from Sadlers Wells Opera and Covent Garden, but other leads and the chorus were drawn from around Devon. When reviewing *Il Trovatore*, Peter Jarman told readers that Devon Opera had a happy family atmosphere, and he was amazed at their singing ability – having no doubt that they could easily fill the Theatre Royal with both sound and audiences.

Frequently there were shows and one-off events staged by other organizations in Exeter's Theatre Royal. However, the various performances by local amateur groups should not be casually mentioned, for many of the so-called amateur performances were as good as, and at times probably better than, quite a few of the professional shows! It is always a special thrill for an amateur company to stage a production to a live audience. For, unlike their professional counterparts, they give their spare time to rehearse and most members are in full time work. To perform on a professional stage gives that extra sparkle to the performance. The school stage, village hall or small, perhaps cramped, town theatre is one thing; the big professional theatre stage is entirely different.

For those amateurs who did entertain at the Theatre Royal, it must have been a very special feeling to give a performance in front of an audience of

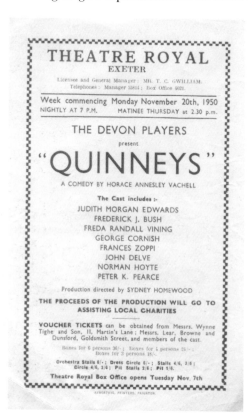

116. Handbill advertising The Devon Players' production of Horace Vachell's Quinneys *in November 1950.*

nearly a thousand, and patrons of amateur shows will have frequently witnessed how professional some amateurs can be. Certainly their enthusiasm and desire to please was at times as strong as that their professional counterparts, and even today it is always a thrill for amateurs to sing, act, or dance on a 'professional' stage.

Some would have already appeared on stage at their school, in village halls, or perhaps their town's theatre. For a few such performers, it was the first step on the ladder to a professional career – and a number of Exeter people have made that important step. Amateur events are always exciting for those on both sides of the proscenium arch, involving that special 'magic' of theatre that is so difficult to explain, but that means as much to an amateur as it does to a hardened professional.

117. The list of theatrical 'digs' available for artistes appearing at the theatre. Prior to gradual redevelopment, there were many roads, squares and terraces in the vicinity of the theatre, and the occupants could generate additional income by offering rooms to let. Some would be basic, but larger houses could sometimes offer a piano for guests to use. This pre-war list was sponsored by Wynne Tighe & Son. Their chemist's shop was in High Street until destroyed in the blitz, when it moved to Martins Lane. Paul Wynne Tighe was a director of the Exeter Theatre Company.

THEATRE ROYAL, EXETER.

LIST OF PROFESSIONAL APARTMENTS.

Those addresses marked with an asterisk have been visited and reported on by a delegate from the Actor's Association, and prices fixed. Artistes are requested not to pay more than the quoted terms, which include fire and lighting.

* MRS ARBERRY.
9 Longbrook Terrace, Exeter.
Bed and Sitting Room (2) 25s. (1) 20s.
Second Set   (2) 20s. (1) 18s.
Combined Room   (2) 18s. (1) 15s.

* MRS. CHANNON
28, Oxford Road.
Bed and Sitting Room (2) 23s. (1) 20s.
Combined Room   (2) 18s. (1) 14s.
Piano

* MRS. COOMBES.
2, St. Sidwell's Terrace.
Bed and Sitting Room (2) 23s. (1) 19s.
Combined Room   (2) 18s. (1) 15s.

MISS DOWN,
14, Poltimore Square.
Bed and Sitting Room (2) 25s. (1) 20s.
Combined Room   (2) 18s. (1) 16s.

* MRS. ELSTON.
89, Paris Street
Bed and Sitting Room (2) 30s. (1) 30s.
Piano, Bath

* MRS. FEATHERSTONE.
1, St. Sidwell's Terrace.
Bed and Sitting Room   (2) 20s.
Combined Room   (2) 16s.

* MRS. HAMSON.
7, Poltimore Square.
Bed and Sitting Room (2) 25s. (1) 20s.
Combined Room   (2) 18s. (1) 15s.

MRS. HAWKINS.
6 Poltimore Square
Combined Room   (2) 18s. (1) 15s.

* MRS. LYONS.
51, Oxford Road.
Bed and Sitting Room (2) 23s. (1) 18s.
Piano.

* MRS. PALTRIDGE.
1, Warren Lane, Longbrook Street.
Bed and Sitting Room (2) 23s. (1) 18s.

* MRS. REEVES.
20, Longbrook Street,
Bed and Sitting Room (2) 23s. (1) 20s.
Combined Room   (2) 18s. (1) 15s.
Piano

* MRS. STENTIFORD.
26, Longbrook Street.
Bed and Sitting Room (2) 22s. (1) 20s.
Combined Room   (2) 18s. (1) 15s.
Piano, Bath

* MRS. SANDERS.
3, St. Sidwells Terrace.
Combined Room   (2) 17s. (1) 14s.

* MRS. SALMON.
17, Poltimore Square.
Bed and Sitting Room (2) 22s. (1) 18s.
Combined Room   (2) 17s. (1) 15s.

* MRS. TRENCHARD.
164a, Fore Street.
Bed and Sitting Room (2) 30s. (1) 25s.
Piano, Bath.

* MRS. TWIGG.
49, Oxford Road.
Bed and Sitting Room (2) 23s. (1) 20s.
Piano

* MRS. TOWNSEND.
63, Oxford Road.
Bed and Sitting Room (2) 23s. (1) 20s.
Piano

* MRS. WHEELAN.
11, North Street.
Bed and Sitting Room (2) 23s. (1) 18s.
Combined Room   (2) 18s. (1) 14s.
Four other Bedrooms
Piano, Bath.

* MRS. SCAGELL.
10, Longbrook Terrace
Bed and Sitting Room (2) 25s. (1) 22s.
Combined Room   (2) 18s. (1) 16s.
Piano, Bath.

THEATRE CARTERS Messrs Pickfords
48, New North Road, Exeter.
Per Load In and Out ...   ... 27s 6d.
Timber Lorries In and Out ... 30s. 0d.

BAGGAGE MEN.
Messrs. Gale and Montandon, Theatre Royal.
    Baskets 1s. 0d. each way
    Bags   ... 6d. each way
St. David's Station (G. W. Ry.) 15 mins.
Queen St. Station (L. and S. W. Ry.) 5 minutes.
(Cross over Bridge into Park for Theatre)
Trams run after 2 p.m. on Sundays.

SUPERS.
2s. 0d. per performance. Super Master 2s. 6d. when more than three supers.

DRESSERS.
1s. 6d. per performance.

TAXIS may be ordered from Messrs. Parker's Garage, St. Sidwell's, Exeter. Messrs. Yeo and Davey, St. Sidwell's, Exeter.

EXETER GOLF LINKS.
9 Holes, 2s. 6d. per day.
Messrs. Yeo and Davey will convey Artistes to the Golf Links at 9d. per person, (minimum of three.)

WYNNE TIGHE & SON,
The Theatrical and Photographic Chemists,
3 & 4, HIGH STREET, EXETER.
(4 Doors below G.P.O.)
FOR ALL THEATRICAL REQUISITES, Etc.

Theatre "Digs"

Wherever there is a Theatre, there has to be accommodation for visiting artistes. Theatre *'digs'* are as important as any other factor for them. The good landlady will provide a suitable haven in which they can relax and be looked after, hopefully, in a home-from-home way. Bad digs will, of course, soon be on the grapevine as a place to avoid. Thus it was in the owners' interests to keep their rooms and establishments to a high standard.

Obviously, the digs have to be as close as possible to the theatre, preferably within a short walking distance, or at least easily reached by public transport. After a tiring day in the theatre, often with a minimum of two matinees a week, artistes will want somewhere close to get back to and rest.

During the existence of the Theatre Royal, there were many digs in and around the Longbrook Street area. The area surrounding the Theatre Royal comprised many streets and terraces, a virtual warren, where occupants of houses were only too pleased to supplement their income with lodgers from the Theatre Royal. Poltimore Square, Warren Lane, Longbrook Street and Longbrook Terrace, Queens Crescent, Church Lane, Howell Road and Oxford Road were all in walking distance, some no longer to be found. When the Theatre advertised for accommodation, as it frequently did, there were numerous replies from existing and potential landladies. Amazingly, some were a considerable distance from the Theatre. For example, during the 1958/59 pantomime season, in addition to the many answers from the Exeter area, replies came from Whitestone, Topsham, Honiton Clyst and Woodbury. Over thirty years ago it would have been difficult reaching these places at about eleven o'clock in the evening. Trains would have been regular to outlying areas, but even then the railway station and the actual house had to be reached. Buses would not have gone that far after 10 pm or thereabouts. Thus the more local landladies stood a better chance of a good 'season' if they provided a clean, comfortable, and reasonably cheap lodging.

Prices were usually quoted in guineas, a guinea being one pound and one shilling, or a pound and five pence today. In the 1940s a week's lodging would

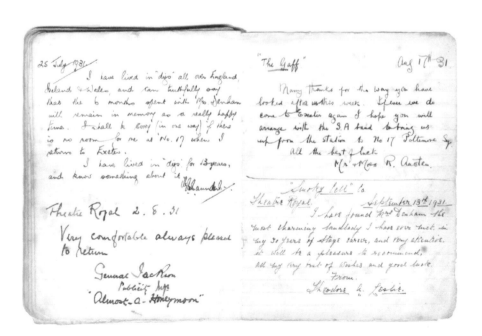

118. *Glowing references in the guest book of Mrs Densham, by actors who took her 'digs' in Poltimore Square, now the site of a multi-storey car park. If the 'digs' were good, artistes would stay there each time they visited the city.*

be in the region of two guineas, full board, and in the 1950s and 1960s it would have varied from 3 to 4 guineas. This must be compared with the average wage of, say, a dancer whose weekly wage was probably not more than £10. Full board would have included a full breakfast if required – the usual eggs, bacon, etc. – and a substantial evening meal. Roast meals and stews were popular, the modern take-away convenience food being unheard of then. On Friday, it was customary for many landladies to provide a fish meal.

Some landladies had visitors' books. Obviously these would contain only good remarks, and often glowing references would be left for others to read. In the late twenties and early thirties a Mrs Densham was a landlady at 17 Poltimore Square, and the remarks in her book suggest that she ran a very popular and acceptable establishment. In 1931 a Mr Sanders spent six months with her, and claimed to have lived in 'digs' for over thirteen years, throughout England, Ireland and Wales, but he rated Mrs Densham's hospitality amongst the best.

The Theatre itself published a list of suitable accommodation addresses, typewritten on foolscap sheets. Slightly more formal was a "List of Professional Apartments" produced by the High Street chemist Wynne Tighe & Son. Most of the prices for a bed and sitting room were around £1 – some slightly more. Some even offer a piano with the accommodation! The list also advised that a dresser could be acquired for 1/6d per performance, and at the Exeter Golf Links, a round of 9 holes would have cost the princely sum of 2/6d. Wynne Tighe had been a well-known chemist, having occupied premises in Martins Lane for many years. Its proprietor, Paul Wynne Tighe, was a director of the Exeter Theatre Company.

The Cinema Screen

In order to maintain a business it is often necessary to diversify. The directors of the Theatre Royal found this necessary when audiences for live shows began to fall off. The popularity of cinema just after the War played its part in attracting audiences away from the live theatre, but another factor was equally, if not more to blame.

The advent of television in the mid-thirties had started to intrigue the population. In the years following the War, television was still in its infancy, but by the early fifties there were several families with this new item of furniture in their lounge. In the early part of the twentieth century, families gathered around the radio set, but the latter part of that century saw families almost ignoring the radio in favour of the 'box'. Theatre was inevitably to suffer, and one way of keeping audiences was to introduce a cinema screen into the theatre and offer another form of entertainment in the same building as the live shows.

Cinema itself was changing, and various forms had been introduced to maintain public interest and attendance. As silent films had given way to 'talkies' with films such as *The Jazz Singer* in 1927, so black and white gave way to colour. Although a trade name, *Technicolour* is the most widely used word to describe the coloured films. For several years film makers never looked back, and after colour came the various forms of cinema which are known today. Wide screen Cinerama, Cinemascope and Todd-AO, three-dimensional (which required

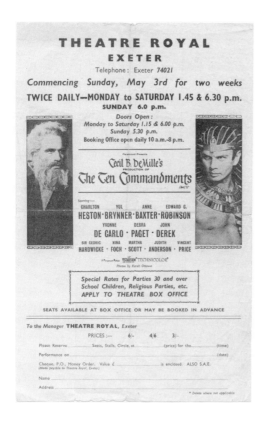

THEATRE ROYAL
EXETER
Telephone: Exeter 74021

special spectacles), and systems such as stereophonic and quadrophonic sound are just some of the improvements tested on cinema patrons.

Audiences packed cinemas in the late forties and early fifties, in particular to see the many films based on the Second World War, some based on true stories, others more fictional. In the early fifties came a spate of British-made films, including the Ealing comedies, beloved by so many people for their simple humour and identifiable situations. It was probably the case that following the hardship and struggles caused by the War and its aftermath, the public wanted something with which they could identify. Something simple which could restore their pride and way of life, and a respite from all they had been through for so many years. The cinema seemed to be able to offer this more than theatres. It was because of the upsurge in cinema audiences around this time that theatres started to follow suit.

In the early part of the twentieth century, films had been shown at the Theatre, in addition to the many live shows. Certainly, in the years leading up to the First World War patrons of the Theatre were able to watch films there. Playbills dating from as early as 1911 advertise cinematographic performances taking place at 7.15 pm each night, before the main show at the Theatre. In 1912, there was advertised "a New Feature, The Gaumont Graphic". This depicted topical events of the week, shown nightly during the interval of the main performance, and changed on Mondays and Thursdays. Was this, perhaps, the forerunner of the Pathe News? At that time private boxes at the rear of the dress circle gave way to a projection room. During the week commencing May 6th 1912, the Theatre management was proud to present 'Selig's great £6,000 film' *Christopher Columbus*, by arrangement with the New Century Film Company.

At the end of 1953 the directors decided to install a large,

119. Films were shown at the theatre as part of the directors' attempts to increase revenue. They had secured a contract with 20th Century Fox, and as a result some first class films were on offer to Exeter's public.

120. Cinema projection equipment in the theatre. This model was a Westar, built by the Westrex company. The large reels of film can be seen at the front of the machine, one at the top and another underneath. Boxes on the walls housed the electrical equipment for controlling the sound faders, change-over shutters and the cinema screen curtains. Just visible on the extreme right is a limelight, or follow spot, used to highlight actors on stage.

121. An early poster for a film at the theatre. In 1925, the 'great Easter attraction' was the showing of The Thief of Bagdad *starring Douglas Fairbanks. The dearest seats in the circle were advertised at 3/6d (17½ pence).*

122. Films were shown at the Theatre Royal in the early part of twentieth century. In 1912 a new feature was advertised, the Gaumont Graphic, *featuring the week's topical events – a forerunner, perhaps, of the Pathé News?*

new screen at the Theatre Royal and once again offer the public films in addition to live shows. In 1954 new Westar film mechanism was installed, together with Peerless lamphouses and a new Western Electrics magnetic sound system. Harry Hopkins was the last Chief Projectionist at the Theatre. He doubled this role with that of Chief Electrician, and recalled an irony in his two jobs; for whilst the stage lighting at the Theatre Royal was some of the oldest in the country, the kinematic projection equipment was, at that time, excellent. Particularly good was the high frequency stereophonic and surround sound installed in the theatre. Although films shown were designed for wide screens, the design of the Theatre Royal interior could not really make the best use of the screen and for patrons in some parts of the auditorium there were viewing difficulties. Harry also recalls that Exeter's theatre had negotiated an agreement with 20th Century Fox to show their latest films in the City. For a long while there had been disputes between the Rank Organisation and 20th Century Fox, mainly regarding the introduction of Cinemascope and stereophonic sound, and for the Theatre to have this new agreement was something of a triumph. The first film shown was *The Robe* in 1954, starring Victor Mature and Richard Burton.

For some years it was a popular attraction, but eventually even cinema fell to the pull of television, and audiences started to dwindle. Although films were shown at the Royal almost right up to the closure, they were not as popular as had been hoped, and latterly were only a way of trying to balance the books. At that time the Theatre was competing with the Odeon, Gaumont and ABC cinemas. Some of the cinematograph equipment from the Theatre Royal was fortunately saved, and can now be seen at the Theatre Museum in Covent Garden, London.

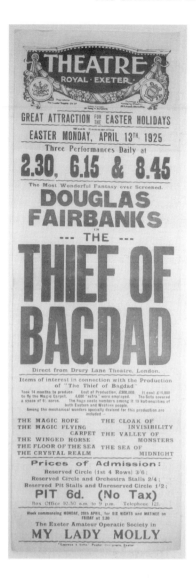

The Theatre Building

The Theatre Royal was situated between two main roadways. New North Road was on one side, and Longbrook Street on the other. New North Road was level, but Longbrook Street dropped considerably from the main entrance to the Theatre, along its whole length. The line of New North Road would have been approximately at the level of the private boxes in the auditorium. Longbrook Street started at virtually the same level as New North Road, but by the time it reached the rear of the Theatre, it was well below the stage level. At the rear of the building was an area, known as Stable Yard, separating the Theatre with the adjacent Blue Star Garage (formerly Maude's City Garages), and it had a considerable slope. So due to the geography of the area, much of the building was partially below ground on the Longbrook Street side, and considerably below ground on the New North Road side.

Patrons, of course, knew the foyer, auditorium and public parts of the Theatre Royal. Few would know of those areas where the public seldom ventured – the stage, the flies, the various stores, prop rooms, dressing rooms, offices and so on. The main entrance was reached from the footpath via a flight of stone steps. Stone steps were to feature elsewhere in the Theatre and were, of course, fireproof. This had been one of the important changes in the rebuilt Theatre. The booking office was on the left just inside the main entrance, with the chocolate kiosk on the right. In addition to the usual seating plans available, the booking office boasted a small model of the Theatre auditorium, enabling patrons to readily identify the seats allocated or chosen. Leading from the foyer was a wide flight of stairs, with heavy carpet and brass handrails, taking patrons to the circle entrances. At the top of the staircase there was usually a large flower arrangement. On the walls hung several framed photographs of previous shows and pantomimes. Wooden part-glazed doors led to the dress circle, and the circle bar, and another flight of stairs led to what was known as the 'Gods', although this only comprised two rows, with a total of 40 seats, and

123. One of the few photographs of the auditorium. On the right hand wall of the dress circle can be seen the large oil paintings depicting local scenes. Originally there were boxes at the rear of the circle, but these were removed to make way for the projection box, seen above the central exit doors. Fittings were mainly brass, including the handrail around the top of the dress circle. Not visible in the photograph, the domed ceiling was decorated in pastel murals.

124. The actress Evelyn Laye pours a drink for manager Cliff Gwilliam in the Circle Bar during one of her visits to the theatre.

a single row of six seats. The single row of six was in front of the projection box (formerly the location of private boxes) that housed the front spotlights, or limes, and later the cinema projectors.

At this level, on the Longbrook Street side, was a long corridor housing the manager's office and several dressing rooms. It is usual for a theatre's Number 1 dressing room to be the 'star' dressing room. In the case of the Theatre Royal, it was dressing room Number 2, for the simple reason it was nearer to the staircase than Number 1, and thus more convenient for the occupant!

The dressing rooms were large and quite well appointed, with ample mirrors, hand basins and plenty of space. In the larger dressing rooms, on the New North Road side, there was also a central hanging rail for costumes to be stored. These rooms were usually occupied by the chorus, or dancers, who often had numerous changes of costume. A problem for them was that these larger rooms were two flights of stairs above the stage. For a quick change this often proved a tiring journey for the hard-working cast!

The dress circle in most theatres is not aptly named, for seldom do they resemble circles in any way. More often they are horseshoe shaped. The dress

125. The box office was located on the left hand side of the foyer. When patrons wished to book seats, there was a model on display to assist them. The model shows seats in the gallery at the rear of the circle, so must have been made prior to 1910 when those seats were removed to house the projection box. The model is now in the author's collection.

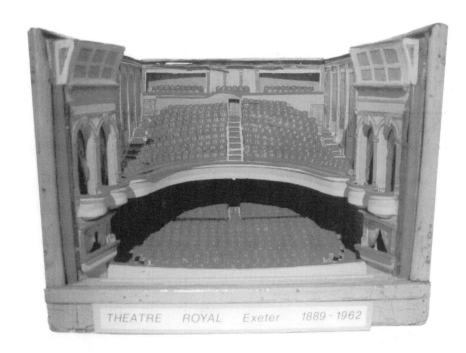

circle at the Royal was actually more an elliptical shape, with the ends of the front two rows being turned out quite sharply. At each end were two boxes, capable of seating up to six persons. They were ideal for those who preferred some privacy at the theatre, but were far from being the 'best' seats, for due to their location the view from each box was extremely restricted. For many years there were also private boxes at the rear of the dress circle, but these were eventually removed to allow for a cinema-style projection box to be constructed.

The whole of the auditorium was quite ornate. The tip-up seats were upholstered and had padded armrests. Brass fittings were in abundance, and the front of the circle had a brass rail around the whole length. The signs directing patrons to the exits, bars, toilets and the like were painted on glass, with brass fixings and brass lamp holders over them. The heating radiators at the sides of the theatre were painted in a gold colour which was reflected in many of the auditorium fittings. The domed ceiling was decorated with murals in pastel shades. Huge framed oil paintings hung on the walls, and at the final auction, some of these oil paintings were sold locally. Originally, four pillars rose from the floor of the pit stalls, supporting the dress circle above. They obviously restricted the view for those who sat behind them, and patrons frequently tried to avoid taking those seats. This situation was improved shortly before the war, in the summer of 1939, when the pillars were removed and massive steel girders installed across the theatre auditorium to support the circle. Despite the fact that this had taken place, it was not unknown for patrons – even to the final years – to request seats that were 'not behind the pillars, please'!

126. Various admission tickets.

The front section of the auditorium, nearest the stage, comprised the pit stalls and orchestra stalls. The latter so named as they were nearest the orchestra pit, separated by a gangway. The orchestra stalls were in one block, and behind this section was another gangway, separating that block from the pit stalls. Unlike the orchestra stalls, this section had a central gangway with seats either side. For many years there was yet another gangway across the theatre, separating the rear six rows of the pit stalls, and this small block was simply known as the pit. Some years after the removal of the pillars, this layout was changed and the gangway disappeared, merging the pit with the pit stalls, although the new layout led to a slight decrease in the number of seats available.

Before the war, on the opening and last nights of the pantomime, the pit stalls and orchestra stalls were all booked as one, presumably to increase revenue as both nights would be completely sold out long before the show opened.

Backstage

When stripped of its scenery, curtains and glitter that the public always see, any theatre stage is a comparatively stark and cold area housing all of the paraphernalia necessary to promote a show. The stage at the Theatre Royal was no different. It could be reached on one side from Stable Yard, off New North Road, or on the other side from Longbrook Street. This latter entrance was the Stage Door entrance, and just inside was the small office of the stage door keeper. To the right was the 'green room' where artistes could rest during performances when they were off stage, and ahead was a gap that formed the entrance to the stage.

At this side of the stage, in the corner, was the electrician's switchboard, from where all the stage lighting was operated. Although not rare, it is quite unusual for a switchboard to be at the side of the stage. Some are on platforms above stage level, and most nowadays will be front-of-house. The front 'lime lights' (formerly worked with actual lime, hence the term) picked out certain people on stage, were powerful lights manually operated from the very back of the auditorium, at the rear of 'the Gods'. Now generally known as follow-spots, as they follow people around the stage, these lamps can be adjusted to give a large pool of light, or reduced to such an extent that just a hand can be illuminated.

Today's theatres are full of electronic wizardry and computerised systems that would have been as impossible to envisage in the early part of the last century as was man walking on the moon. The Theatre Royal switchboard was huge compared with modern systems, and lights were literally switched on and off as one does in a private residence. The amount of light available from each lamp was controlled by a system of copper plates being immersed into salt water held in conical containers below stage, but operated by the electrician from on stage. The chemical reaction of the plates coming closer together, or going away from each other varied the brightness of the lights. This had been standard practice for many years in most theatres, but the Theatre Royal was thought to have been the last major theatre to have continued using the system, although many smaller theatres probably did so many years after. The press of

*127. The lighting
switchboard, located in the
wings of the stage. Harry
Hopkins (on the right) was
the last chief electrician
and projectionist.*

a button to carry out such lighting control was then in its infancy – and for a microchip to control the fading out of a light over a determined time was, in those days, beyond comprehension!

At the rear of the stage was a scene dock, for storing scenery, and from here a stone step led up to the props room. It was in this wonderfully magic area of untidiness and chaos that were housed all manner of properties needed on stage. Over the years, little had been discarded. Pantomime props such as oversized papier-mâché joints of meat, suitcases that fall apart, Cinderella's glass slipper, large imitation bottles of sweets, car horns, huge dog bones, oversize eggs and cotton wool snowballs. Standard props such as lamp standards, tables, mirrors, vases, stools, chairs or a fire grate that looks as if it is glowing – all had their place in that room, waiting to be brought into use on stage. Leading from the props room was a door into a scenery store, from where a metal staircase led to the paint room, where much of the theatre scenery was painted.

The stage was of timber, and much of the scenery had to be fixed to make it stand upright. The method was to fix an adjustable 'brace' with a screw-eye (a large screw with a ring instead of a slotted head) screwed into the back of the scenery. A stage screw (a large screw with a triangular head into which a hand could be placed to turn it) would be put through a metal foot on the brace, and screwed into the stage itself. If the scene change was required quickly, then a 56 pound weight would be used instead of the screw. Obviously a wooden stage suffers considerable wear and tear, and after some 59 years of continual usage, in 1948 the Directors engaged a local contractor to replace the entire stage floor. The cost was £259, and the whole operation took just three days – Good Friday, Saturday and Easter Sunday.

The stage was just short of thirty feet in width, and fifty-four feet deep. The proscenium arch was twenty-three feet high. To the side of the stage, opposite to the switchboard, was the operating area for the main curtain. This was worked manually, as many still are. This was also the corner where the 'prompt' sat – a person following the script to prompt any of the cast who forgot their lines. The right hand side of the stage (looking from the audience) is the 'prompt'

128. Stage manager David Edmund, centre, with stagehands Chris Stabb (left) and Ron Tuson, setting scenery in readiness for a show. Behind David are large floodlights that stood in the wings to illuminate scenery.

side, and the left hand side 'opposite prompt'. Underneath the stage was a small office for the stage manager, a band room, and the entrance to the orchestra pit for the musicians. The under-stage area was also an occasional working area for stagehands, for here were two important aspects of the Theatre.

Although not in common usage during the latter years of the Theatre's existence, trap doors in the stage had at one time been used a great deal – especially in pantomime. In those days, the Demon King would suddenly shoot up 'through' the stage, accompanied by the usual smoke and flash. This was accomplished by a spring-loaded trap door, with the King – or whoever – having to stand on an exact spot to avoid a very nasty accident as he or she was propelled aloft!

The main reason for anyone working under the stage was that here was housed an extremely cumbersome winch that raised and lowered the safety curtain. Safety curtains were made of a fireproof material, and such was the weight of the Theatre Royal safety curtain (some four tons) that it required four men to work the winch – two on either side of the handles. This curtain had, by law, to be brought in at least once during every performance, and to give it a more attractive appearance, it was also used as an advertisement board. Those working the winch had no easy task, and were required to work as a team, concentrating on keeping the winch working at a constant pace, otherwise the curtain would not come in smoothly. Having successfully winched it in, a few minutes later it was winched out again!

In the wings, on the New North Road side, were the massive 'elephant doors' leading to Stable Yard. These doors were so named because they were suitably constructed to allow circus animals, including elephants, on to the stage area. Although the stage was supported from underneath by pillars, in the rare event of a circus coming to the Theatre, these pillars had to be augmented with numerous additional props. The reason being that there was a natural 'spring' to the stage due to its construction, and although this would not normally be noticeable when people were walking over it, an elephant's weight would cause the stage to move slightly and these animals will not walk on any surface unless it feels sound to them. Thankfully elephants were not a common occurrence on stage!

In any large professional theatre, working backstage has never been an easy task. Even in today's modern theatre, much work is carried out manually, although it has to be said that there are now far more technical aids. Computers have, of course, made great advances and theatres have reaped the benefit. Hours of work have been eliminated by the mere press of a button or the flick of a switch.

Sometimes routine, even boring, every new show at the Theatre Royal, or indeed any theatre, was different for the stagehands. New routines had to be followed, entirely different scenery had to be set, and the job being done on Saturday night was frequently completely different to that of the following Monday. Much effort went into ensuring that each show was the best. In the same way that an audience will be quick to criticise a poor performance on stage, it will also be equally critical of slipshod scenery changing. The smooth progress of a show was very much in the hands of the Stage Manager and his team.

It is not possible, in such a short space, to explain fully how backstage teams work, nor is it necessary. The Theatre Royal was first and foremost a professional theatre. It was essential, therefore, that the backstage team knew exactly what they were required to do: work quietly, in virtual darkness, and be prepared to react to one person's instructions, whether they were right or wrong. Speed and silence were of great importance – but that, at times, could be far from easy to achieve.

Many patrons did not realise, for example, that the stage of the Theatre Royal had what is known as a 'rake'. That is to say the whole stage sloped from the back to the front, and the slope was considerable. Downstage, the height from the stage floor to the top of the proscenium arch was just over twenty-three feet. Upstage (that is the very rear of the stage) the height was just under twenty two feet, a difference of almost eighteen inches. This could often cause problems in the setting of a show – for instance in shows using revolving sets ice rinks or in 'spectaculars' such as Curries Waterfalls. Some scenery had to be constructed specially to allow for the rake.

Due to the height of the proscenium arch it was necessary for some sets to have scenery twenty feet in height – and some pieces of scenery were about six feet in width, but on occasions even wider. Such pieces were not necessarily

129. Stage manager Charlie Hutchings retired in 1956 and handed over the role of stage manager to David Edmund. Charlie is seen centre, with some of his team.

From the left: Bert Reynolds, Charlie Baker, Tommy Hutchings, Charlie, Reg Harvey, (not identified), Ron Tuson, Ben Northcott, David Edmund, (not identified), Bert Lee.

130. The stagehands take a well-earned rest for a photograph in 1960!

Back row L-R: Chris Stabb; Charlie Tudball; (unidentified); Tommy Hutchings; David Edmund; Bert Lee; Stuart Patten; Peter Jarman.

Front row L-R: Dick Hutchings; Ron Tuson; Reg Harvey; Johnny Johnson; Pip ?; Ben Northcott; Bert Reynolds (half hidden)

heavy, but cumbersome. To manhandle scenery that size, quietly and in very subdued lighting, was certainly no easy task, yet it was carried out night after night with only the occasional major hitch.

Much scenery was in the form of backcloths, either the full width and depth of the stage, or cut out to give some perspective to a full cloth. Woodland scenes would usually have a full cloth at the back, with one or two additional cut cloths, perhaps depicting overhanging branches, hung in front of the main cloth to give a feeling of depth – a form of three dimensional scenery. These cloths were of a hessian-type material and hung on long wooden battens, with a smaller metal bar, or some form of weighting, sewn into the bottom edge, to make the cloth hang correctly.

Three hemp ropes would be tied to the bar – one at each end and one in the centre. These were known as the long, middle and short (the 'long' and 'short' depending from which side of the stage the flymen were working). To move a cloth in or out, it would have to be hauled manually by the flymen who were perched on a platform high above the side of the stage. On a signal from below, perhaps a click of the fingers or subdued whistle from the Stage Manager, they would haul hand over hand. For heavy cloths or scenery this would necessitate sometimes two men, or more, who would haul away until the cloth was 'in' on the stage or 'out', high above the stage and out of sight for the audience. In those days it was sheer hard work – with no electrical assistance or counterweighted pulley systems to assist the haul.

Sets were usually made of a wooden frame with hessian stretched over it, covered with size and then painted (in a special scenic paint) with whatever was required as the scene. For some shows, scenery would also be fixed to a bar and hauled in and out. There could be perhaps doors built into the scenery, or windows, fireplaces, etc. The weight of such a scene would be enormous, and the flymen and stage crew needed to be strong and fit.

It was not just the scenery that required moving during a show. The stage was 'dressed' by the Property Master and his, or her, team. Tables, chairs, sofas, trays with real glasses of liquid, vases of flowers, newspapers, envelopes to be opened and a letter read out, pictures to be hung on walls – all manner of little items which go to make up a scene have to be put on stage – and in the right place!

Sometimes it may only be for a few minutes, and then everything has to be moved off again. From huge settees to small personal items – all have to be in position on stage in time for the scene to open, for without a certain 'prop' an actor could lose his lines or miss an entrance. There is little point in ringing for the butler if the bell has been forgotten! Similarly, the butler cannot remove a tray if it has not been set in the first instance! They may seem minor, but are imperative details.

In professional shows, a dresser may be at hand to assist artistes changing in the wings. For a costume change, each article of clothing has to be ready for the actor to come off stage and change into, usually very quickly and sometimes with more than one person having to change. All this action – scene changing, props being moved to and fro, and costumes being changed – is often being carried out at the same time whilst another scene is being played. Once again, speed and silence are essential. Add to that the actors and actresses needing perhaps to enter and exit, or a chorus trying to get on quickly. It is not difficult to understand why there is a great need for discipline and mutual understanding backstage.

Many more people are also involved in some way. In earlier days, a call boy would often be used to warn actors when their entrance is due, though more frequently these days it is done by way of a tannoy system in the dressing rooms. The Theatre Royal used a tannoy system with speakers in all dressing rooms, the cast being 'called' from a microphone at the side of the stage. Cues are also a vital part of any show. Lighting technicians will require cues to change the lighting, as will sound engineers to bring in a certain sound effect. Flymen will await cues before they haul cloths in and out from their position over the stage. Calling and cueing will usually be the job of an assistant stage manager working to one side of the stage, out of sight of the audience but with a good view of what is happening on stage.

To watch a show from the wings for the first time would probably give the impression of a chaotic shambles to many; but out of that apparent disorder there is a well-rehearsed routine to ensure that the show, seen from the other side of the curtain, runs as smoothly as possible. The scenery and props (known as 'the set') for a show would usually be hired from specialist companies, or brought to the Theatre by the company performing that week – although on occasions some were constructed at the Theatre by the stage team, under the direction of the stage carpenter. The scenery would naturally depend of the type and size of show. A play could be just one act, requiring a very small set –

131. Offloading scenery at the stage door in Longbrook Street. 30 feet long flats are rolled up on top of a lorry load of 'flats' – pieces of scenery 20 feet high and at least six feet wide. The shop on the right no longer exists.

whereas scenery for a variety show would be changing every ten minutes or so. The set for an average show would consist of several 'flats' and cloths, with numerous other smaller pieces of scenery, plus wicker skips of props and costumes. The *flats,* those large pieces of scenery mentioned earlier, could number twenty or thirty for just one show – or even more for a large show or pantomime. The theatre stage manager was responsible for organising the trains to be met and offloaded, and for the scenery to be transported to and from the Theatre.

For large touring companies, and for other special one-off shows at the Royal, scenery would have to brought in, and the standard way of transporting it then was by rail, and then by lorry to the theatre. For many years Pickfords had the haulage contract for the Theatre Royal, and as they had a store just around the corner of Longbrook Terrace, they were most conveniently situated. It was quite a slick operation, involving many people and much work. All the scenery would be collected from St David's station and delivered to the side entrance in Longbrook Street. Sometimes a side alley between the Theatre and Blue Star Garages in New North Road would be used, by way of the 'elephant doors' entrance.

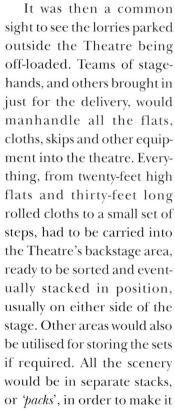

132. Scenery and backcloths being offloaded and taken on to the stage by way of the stage door in Longbrook Street.

It was then a common sight to see the lorries parked outside the Theatre being off-loaded. Teams of stage-hands, and others brought in just for the delivery, would manhandle all the flats, cloths, skips and other equipment into the theatre. Everything, from twenty-feet high flats and thirty-feet long rolled cloths to a small set of steps, had to be carried into the Theatre's backstage area, ready to be sorted and eventually stacked in position, usually on either side of the stage. Other areas would also be utilised for storing the sets if required. All the scenery would be in separate stacks, or *'packs'*, in order to make it easier and quicker to set a scene. It is usual for each side of the stage to have scenery that would be set that side. Hopefully, on coming came to the last piece, it should meet up with the opposite side's last piece!

The offloading was frequently done early on a Sunday morning, followed by what is known as a 'fit up', when all the scenery is set in position and marked, all the cloths hung, and all the legs and borders (which mask the gaps between pieces of scenery) put in place. If there was any form of rehearsal on the Sunday evening, which was not usual, but did happen from time to time, the day could be quite long for the stagehands. On rare occasions, the set would arrive on a Monday morning and this meant setting 'last first'. The final set would be arranged on stage first, the positions of each piece of scenery marked and then the next scene would be set likewise. This working backwards continued until the first scene was set in position, and that would then be left for the opening of the show. If the show had one two or three scenes, there may have been time for some rehearsal. Frequently on such occasions the first scene would have been finally set only an hour or so before curtain up, allowing no time for rehearsal on stage.

At the end of the week, or at the end of a show's run, the reverse procedure would apply. After the final performance, all the cloths would be taken down, and the scenery dismantled. Costumes would be carefully packed back into the wicker skips, and any props that came with the scenery stored together. Frequently many items required as props would be obtained locally. These would be separated and returned to their source of origin. Everything having been dismantled and brought together, it was then loaded onto lorries in the early hours of the morning, ready for the railway station, although sometimes the scenery would have been taken by road. At Exeter St David's, the scenery would be loaded into specially allocated trucks that had end-loading facilities, making it much easier to load. The scenery would be carried through each truck, so that when the first was full, the second would be used, and when that was full the next – until each truck was full of scenery. This was all carried out at a separate siding, still in use today, to prevent any disruption of normal train services. Once loaded onto the appropriate train, everything would be sent back to the hiring company, or possibly to be forwarded to the next theatre – be it Torquay or Edinburgh. At its destination the whole procedure would start again!

The Demise

Following the destruction of Exeter's centre during the bombing raids of 1942, the city council commissioned town planner Thomas Sharp to put forward plans for rebuilding. One proposal concerned the Theatre Royal. A report in the *Express & Echo* of December 28th 1945 stated that Exeter was preparing 'to make a really historic resolution'. The report of plans to 'create a new city, that will be beautiful, airy and well and spaciously planned to meet future requirements'. Thomas Sharp was quoted as saying that, 'with some regret', he would suggest a new location for the Theatre Royal. He proposed that the Theatre should be relocated to a new principal town square, to be constructed around the existing, but severely damaged, London Inn Square in the city centre. 'Exeter', he said, 'was lucky to maintain a theatre of its own which was rather remarkable for a city of its size'. His proposal was that the existing theatre be demolished and a new building erected just a few yards away. That proposal, however, was not followed.

Some fifteen years later, with the start of the nineteen sixties, theatre in general was facing its own problems, and Exeter's own theatre was not without its share. The Annual Meeting of the shareholders of the Exeter Theatre Company, in November 1959, certainly reinforced that. Sir Leonard Costello, the acting chairman, painted a grim picture of the Theatre's financial position.

EXETER THEATRE SOLD TO

NEW OFFICES TO BE BUILT ON SITE

PRUDENTIAL: £85,000

THE Theatre Royal, Exeter, has been purchased by the Prudential Assurance Company Ltd. for £85,000, it was announced today.

A spokesman for the company in London told the "Express & Echo" that they intended to erect a new building on the site for their own use. It was hoped to make a further statement in about a month's time. It is understood that planning consent for a new building has been granted by Exeter City Council.

The Prudential have been in Exeter about 50 years. Staff moves from their present offices in Cathedral Yard to the new building, possibly regional offices, would be probable. The building would be comparable in design to other new development in the vicinity, it is believed, but not as high as the nearby Bobby's building now under construction.

The deal does not include the effects of the theatre, which will be sold separately.

The sale has been made "by virtue of the directors' inherent powers" following a resolution passed at the extraordinary general meeting of the Exeter Theatre Company on August 30.

Sir Leonard Costello (chairman of the board) said at today's Press conference announcing the sale: "There are two things I am sure the general public does not altogether appreciate. One is that this company, although it is intended to be a profit-making concern, has, in fact, made no profit since 1955, and consequently the shareholders have received no return for their capital since that year.

'Public service'

"It also has to be remembered that this company is a rarity, if not unique, in as much that, though it is intended to be a profit-making company, the directors have never had or asked for any remuneration—not because there was no money, but because they have always regarded it as a matter of public service.

"It has always been their endeavour to give this service to the city and surrounding countryside for the benefit of the public generally. I can say unhesitatingly that the directors of this company have so regarded their duties and have thought it a privilege to have the opportunity of serving society in this kind of way.

MR. CLIFF GWILLIAM, the managing director of the theatre, told the "Express and Echo" that he was seriously considering an invitation to join the board of the Palace, Plymouth. He believed that Plymouth would be the future centre of entertainment in the Westcountry. The Palace—closed for sometime—was reopened about a year ago when it was bought by four local businessmen.

"Therefore one is naturally inclined to feel hurt if and when there is any kind of unwarranted criticism—or, of course, unjustifiable abuse."

The second important point was that the directors, in pursuance of what they regarded as a privilege and trust, had done their utmost in the past three or four years to maintain the theatre as a live theatre.

"I am quite sure that all of us have been single-minded about this. Our one desire has been to keep the theatre going, but the board has not been supported by people outside."

Sir Leonard referred to the Prudential's figure as "a handsome one." And then he referred to the extraordinary meeting of shareholders which had been requisitioned "by a certain number of shareholders" for next month.

"This requisition was not lodged with us until October 11—a week after there had been an offer and acceptance with the Prudential," said Sir Leonard. "This place was morally sold at that date.

"One can only hope that those people who, according to their ideals, have done their best to 'save the theatre,' may now come to the conclusion that it would be futile and beating the air to come to a meeting at all," he added.

He said that the shareholders in question had put forward no practical suggestions to the board, though everything possible had been done to frustrate the considered opinions of the board.

Sir Leonard said it had been alleged that there was a demand for a poll at the last meeting, but as far as they could see there had been, only two shareholders demanding this and not the three required by law. The resolution to sell the theatre on the most advantageous terms" had been passed on a clear show of hands.

The bank had made it abundantly clear that no more money was forthcoming from that quarter and the company promised on its honour to close the theatre on September 22—which it did.

THREE TIMES SHARE VALUE

Mr. H. T. Howe, deputy chairman of the theatre company, said this afternoon that ordinary shareholders would get three or four times the value of their shares because of the sale.

But, he added, there were many shareholders who hoped never to see what had happened come to pass. "They would willingly have given shares for the continuance of the theatre as a theatre. It is a terribly sad day for the city. I am sure something could have been done if only the city council and the Northcott Trust representatives had got together."

133. The Express & Echo *reports on the sale for £85,000 to the Prudential Assurance Company.*

He stated that the position had become 'really acute', adding that the Company was 'in desperate straits'. If the current financial situation did not improve, he could not foresee any possibility of the Theatre surviving more than a few weeks after the forthcoming pantomime – which would have been early in 1960. In June 1959, the annual report had shown a deficit of £1,016. Such was the seriousness of the following few months that a further financial report was prepared in October, but was not made available to the press and the details are not known. That second report must have made grim reading, for Sir Leonard stated that the company may not have any other option than to consider a sale.

Mr George Butt, one of the shareholders and a well known local figure, informed the meeting that he had seen an Exeter building advertised for sale and on receiving the estate agent's details he was amazed to see that it described the Theatre Royal. The directors immediately denied any responsibility for authorizing such an advertisement, and Mr Gwilliam, the Theatre manager, said that no member of the company was responsible, although he did add that he had received numerous enquiries from people wishing to buy the site and premises. There followed much debate, and Mr James Whiteside stated that he considered the matter 'to be of extreme gravity', and proposed 'a rigorous investigation'. Such was the feeling, that the meeting was adjourned for a week for investigations to be made into Mr Butt's statement.

The matter was quickly resolved. Whilst it may have been strictly correct to say that no director had specifically *authorised* the advertisement, Mr Gwilliam's remark that 'no member of the Company was responsible' is a little more questionable. At the adjourned meeting the following week, it transpired that two Directors, Ald. W. Hill (the company chairman) and Col. W. Symes (the secretary) had asked Cliff Gwilliam to make 'tentative and discreet enquiries'

THE EXETER THEATRE COMPANY LIMITED

NOTICE OF EXTRA-ORDINARY GENERAL MEETING

NOTICE is hereby given that an Extra-ordinary General
Meeting of The Exeter Theatre Company Limited will be held
on Thursday, 30th August, 1962, at 11 a.m. at the Theatre
Royal, Exeter, for the purpose of considering the Directors'
report on the negotiations recommended by the Shareholders
at the Adjourned Extra-ordinary General Meeting held on
Monday, 14th May, 1962, and to pass the following Resolution
unanimously approved by the Directors of the Company and
strongly recommended to the Shareholders for acceptance.

THAT the Shareholders of the Company
hereby empower the Board of Directors forth-
with to negotiate a sale of all the assets
of the Company and to sell the same upon the
most advantageous terms.

Every Member entitled to attend and vote at this Meeting
can, if he/she so desires, appoint a Proxy to attend and vote
in his/her stead and such Proxy need not be a member of the
Company.

L. SEARLE SMALE,
Secretary.

30. 7. 62.

134. The notice of an Extra-Ordinary General Meeting of the Exeter Theatre Co. Ltd., called for August 1962, informing shareholders of another proposed resolution to sell "upon the most advantageous terms". A similar resolution in 1960 had been rejected.

as to the current value of the Theatre building. This he did by approaching a Newton Abbot estate agency, and although that firm was responsible for the advertisement that Mr Butt had seen, the two directors who instigated the valuation – and also, perhaps, Mr Gwilliam as a fellow director – must be expected to share some of the responsibility.

It was perhaps unfortunate for them not to have admitted any involvement, rather than allow the board to issue a statement of denial. Whilst the two concerned may not have given authorization for any adverts, and possibly not even been asked to do so, is it not reasonable to expect an estate agent to ''test the water" by placing such an advertisement? Yet why go out of Exeter in the first place? Virtually all members of the board of directors were responsible and successful business people, and surely amongst their colleagues in the city were many who could have been approached privately for an opinion as to the market value of the building? The somewhat surreptitious approach to obtaining a valuation suggested that a sale of the Theatre was uppermost in the mind of the directors involved. As the shareholders learned the facts, there was obvious resentment at what had taken place, many considering the attitude of the board 'a little too casual'. Mr James Whiteside, a firm supporter of preventing the Theatre from being sold, proposed that the inquiry results be accepted "with some dissatisfaction", and the meeting agreed to look into ways of saving the Theatre.

Despite this, it was at the beginning of February in 1960, that the directors of the Exeter Theatre Company came to their shareholders with a resolution 'to close the Theatre Royal at the earliest opportunity to avoid further losses, and to negotiate the sale of all the assets of the Company...'. At that meeting there was much debate as to whether it was the right thing to do, whether alternatives were possible, or whether the Board were being hasty. The minutes show there was considerable lobbying on both sides, with several prominent Exeter personae having their say. Alderman Charles Hill moved the resolution, but Mr Steele-Perkins suggested voluntary liquidation, supported by Mr George Butt. Mr James Whiteside strongly urged that a further period of twelve months should elapse before anything final was decided. Mr Stanley Stokes agreed with this suggestion. Further comments were voiced by Lt. Col. Creasy, Freda Randall-Vining, Leonard Crump, and Alderman Walter Daw, all of whom demanded a review in twelve months. Finally their request was granted and a large majority of shareholders voted in favour of a further year's trial. As a result, an exasperated Alderman Hill, the Chairman, stated that he was "unable to stand the continual worry of the situation" and he wished to resign. Col. Symes also stated he intended to resign. Mr Leonard Crump urged that 'the sniping at one another, and the continual rocking of the boat' should stop. He added that 'now was the time to pull together, not for mass resignations'.

Despite the shareholders' victory, other desperate survival attempts, and much debate within the pages of local newspapers, the fate of the Theatre seemed inevitable. Meetings came and went during the early part of 1962, but in August yet another shareholders' meeting was presented with a similar resolution to close the Theatre and sell the company assets. At a meeting of the shareholders in late August, described by the *Express & Echo* as being "stormy", Sir Leonard Costello, the chairman of the board of directors, reported that the Theatre was losing £1,000 each month. He said that the Company's liabilities were £34,217 and the bank overdraft was £30,370, against £17,721 at the same time the previous year.

On this occasion the directors got their wish, and towards the end of 1962 the Theatre Royal, Exeter, lowered its curtain for the final time. No more would the spotlights pierce the gloom; no more would that special sound of a theatre orchestra waft over the

135. A worker stands silhouetted against the backdrop of the auditorium during the demolition process.

auditorium; and no more would the sound of applause ring in an artiste's ears from within those walls. On Saturday 22nd September, Clarkson Rose brought the summer season run of *Twinkle* to an end. At the close of the final show, the cast stood on stage taking their traditional last-night bow. Bobby Dennis, Frankie Holmes, Pauline Ashley, Bill Cameron, Marilyn Wildman, Brian Handley, the Clarkson Rosebuds together with the rest of the cast – and of course 'Clarkie' himself – all enjoyed the applause of what was to be the last audience in the Theatre Royal. Somewhat ironically, and certainly not created because of the impending closure, the final sketch of the show involved the whole company, and was entitled "Don't let's say goodbye".

136. In November 1962, Exeter citizens were confronted by Express & Echo *posters proclaiming the sale. An era had ended.*

Twinkle's finale was that of the Theatre Royal also; following the usual thanks, Cliff Gwilliam paid his final tribute to, again ironically, a capacity audience. The orchestra played the National Anthem for the last time and the audience left the building. Whatever 'twinkle' there was had now been extinguished forever.

Just two months after the Theatre finally closed, Messrs Sanders and Redfern commenced the auction of the entire contents at 11am on Wednesday, 21st November. Later that month there followed another auction at Eastmond's yard in Exwick, when "timber and demolition materials from the Theatre Royal" were sold by Messrs Husseys Ltd. This sale included joists, flooring, slates, windows etc., and no doubt there are buildings around the city constructed with some of the materials.

The Theatre Royal, Exeter, died – some would possibly say it had been killed off. What had undoubtedly been an 'institution' in the city ceased, and yet again the Exeter public were, for a short while, denied live theatre. During the period when it became known that the Theatre Royal was to be sold, there was much debate on the reasons. Lack of money, the rise of television popularity, bad management, poor audiences and many other reasons were put forward.

Several were demonstrative in their bids to save the Theatre from closing. Victor Pinckney, a local businessman, had leaflets printed urging patrons to protest to their local councilors regarding the closure, and he personally stood outside the Theatre, distributing them to the departing audiences. A lady was particularly 'exasperated at the manner in which the Theatre has been sold for demolishment'. Her fury was aimed at the directors, in particular Sir Leonard Costello. She daubed slogans in paint on the Theatre walls in the early hours of one morning, and when apprehended by a passing police officer, she told him that 'he deserved it', and asked him if she could finish off her slogans on the wall in Longbrook Street! The chairman of the magistrates (Mrs M. Hesse) told her that 'her very stupid behaviour' deserved the maximum penalty of £5! Many letters were sent to the local *Express & Echo* concerning the whole subject of the closure, some for and some against. Miss Gill Brown, of Chudleigh, even wrote slogans in lipstick on her car, in what she described as 'her one woman campaign to keep alive the Theatre Royal'.

It is regrettable that, on many occasions, audiences dwindled to a mere handful. That, of course, does not assist good budgeting. There can be no doubt that audience numbers did play a large part in the directors' decision to sell. However, many people would say that the wrong types of show were engaged, not those that the public wanted to see. Other more important factors were also to swing the balance towards closure. Water passes under bridges, and it is perhaps too late now to argue the reason for the Theatre Royal to go so ingloriously.

If there were ever any reasons which were not made public, then we shall never know; and if so, perhaps now that is just as well. Debate will doubtless continue for many more years, especially if a new theatre is forthcoming; but no matter what the reason, the old building has gone forever, and cannot be resurrected. Nevertheless, and contrary to this line of thinking, in writing the history of an institution such as the Theatre Royal, it is right to remind the reader of one or two salient facts, without prolonging the argument too long.

The reason for selling was put down to the financial position confronting the directors during the three or four seasons before 1962. It would seem, from reports circulated in the Press, and statements made by some of the board, the Company's financial state was such that to carry on would have possibly meant the Exeter Theatre Company knowingly trading as an insolvent company. That, of course, would have been illegal and could not be allowed. The Company's bankers were said to have refused them further money.

From the annual directors' reports it becomes fairly clear that for many years leading up to the Second World War, the Theatre ran with a small profit. From 1929 until 1939 every year showed a profit. In the financial year 1929/30 it was £2,715, in 1933/34 it fell to £560, in 1936/37 the profits rose to £2,195 and the year before the outbreak of war showed a reasonable sum (for that time) of £1,253. Whilst these sums may now seem small, it has to be remembered that the period covered is between sixty and seventy years ago.

During the war years many papers were allegedly lost. The directors reported they were concerned at the actions of Mr J. P. G.Davey, who was secretary, chairman and managing director of the Exeter Theatre Company. He had apparently refused to call meetings and deliver proper accounts. His actions were supported by a fellow director, Mr Fred Jerman. Counsel was instructed and for some two years the Board was engaged in legal wrangling, culminating in the matter being taken to the High Court in 1944. Various resolutions were then proposed to oust Davey and Jerman, and eventually both were replaced. The Board was once more in control, but there are no records for the major part of the war years.

For the next few years profits were made – in 1944/45 £1,593; 1946/47 £2,543; 1947/48 £2,822. It was not until the early part of the nineteen fifties that profits dwindled. From 1950 until 1953 the company made less than £1000, and the records show that in June of 1950 the profit was a mere £202. For the rest of 1950 there was some improvement, and Cliff Gwilliam is on record as having claimed that during 1950 there were 27,000 more patrons than in 1949. In the year ending 1953 there was a loss of £1,698. In the year 1953/54 the loss had increased to a staggering £4,922 and in 1954/55 it was £1,837. The following year showed a loss of £1,787, although it would then appear that the Company's fortunes had turned again, for 1956/57 showed a fairly healthy profit. This could have been partly as a result of films being shown at the Theatre, for it was during 1954 that the Theatre secured the exclusive rights to show 20th Century Fox cinemascope films.

In the *Express & Echo* of November 1st 1962, Sir Leonard Costello was quoted as saying that although one object of the company was to make a profit, 'none had been made since 1953'. He is also alleged to have claimed that none of the directors had received any remuneration as no money was available. Whilst this was perhaps somewhat unusual for a company, it was probably correct as all of the directors wanted to see the Theatre survive. By not taking any remuneration they helped the critical state of the finances. However, his remarks regarding profit perhaps need closer scrutiny, for the directors' report to the annual meeting of the Exeter Theatre Company in 1957 clearly stated 'It is with some satisfaction that the Directors can place before the Shareholders for the first time in four years a profit of £1,410'.

In the following year, 1958, the directors' report opens with the news of 'a profit of £2,314 having been made after the cost of re-seating the circle for the sum of £1,405'. This report was dated 28th October 1958. No doubt an accountant, having studied the full balance sheets, would immediately come forward with an explanation, but to the layman the profit of 1957 had almost been doubled in 1958, and had the circle not been improved the profit would have been approaching three times that of 1957. There appears to be some discrepancy between the statement by Costello, and the directors' reports. Was there no profit made after 1953, or were the reports of 1957 and 1958 somewhat misleading?

The figures were set out in the annual balance sheets and it is unlikely that Sir Leonard Costello, a man of considerable standing and a well-known persona in Exeter, would have deliberately sought to mislead his shareholders. Why, then, was he reported as saying that there had been no profit since 1953, and why would that have been reported if not true? That question aside, over the next three years any financial success there had been in 1957 and 1958 appears

*137. The poster
advertising the sale of
contents by Messrs Sanders
and Redfern.*

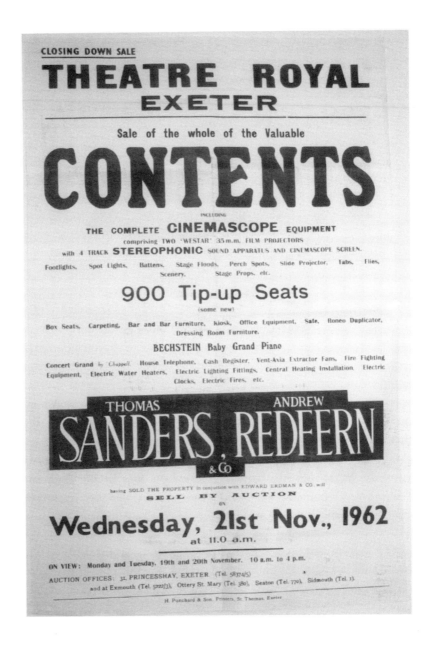

to have been wiped out, for in June 1959 the accounts showed a loss of £1,016. In 1960 the loss jumped to a massive £6,500 – the highest ever. The following year, which was to be the penultimate year of the Theatre's existence, saw a loss of just £1,400.

Despite the fact that there were losses in the middle fifties, and that businesses were at that time still struggling to overcome the disastrous war years, no suggestion appears to have been made then that the Theatre should be closed. In fact the director's report for June 1958 suggests that by considering the circle worth improving during that year, there were no thoughts of the theatre closing down, for otherwise they surely would not have authorized the £1,400 on re-seating. The only 'great concern' they expressed was over the inevitable rise in salaries. Yet a mere three years later, and not long after at least two years of reasonable profits, it was the opinion of the directors that to continue trading would have been impossible. No doubt the staggering loss of 1960 was fresh in their minds. Sir Leonard Costello told shareholders that the minimum weekly cost of running the Theatre was around £400, but the

Company was not able to generate that amount of money each week. It was alleged that the Theatre was suffering losses of around £1,000 per month. It was considered, therefore, that in fairness to the company shareholders the Theatre building should be sold. These figures, profits and losses may now seem incredibly small and perhaps insignificant, but as stated elsewhere, it has to be remembered that they refer to accounts and business transactions of some fifty years ago.

During the discussions regarding the Theatre's future at meetings of shareholders, various options were apparently open. Early in 1962 an offer to purchase the Theatre outright and continue running it as a provincial theatre had been received by Cliff Gwilliam. He refused to disclose the name of the London impresario making the offer, but claimed he represented people "of high standing in the entertainment industry". That offer was never taken further by the board. The company received another offer, from Capitol and Provincial Theatres, to lease the building and again continue its use as a Theatre and run classic cinemas, as they did in twenty-eight other venues throughout the country. This offer had, it was claimed, arrived 48 hours after the agreement to sell was signed, and the directors could not go back on that agreement. Capitol's offer is said to have been a sum of £20,000, plus £1,400 per annum rental for a period of fourteen years.

It was, in fact, Cliff Gwilliam – a director as well as the Theatre manager – who put forward a resolution that the Theatre should be offered for sale on 'the most advantageous terms'. It would appear that the Prudential Assurance Company had come forward with such terms and the directors eventually agreed to sell for £85,000, a figure that today seems very little for such a prominent site in the city centre. One somewhat strange fact regarding the decision to sell is that the resolution was approved at an extraordinary meeting of the shareholders on August 30th 1962. The ordinary members of the Theatre Company, however, were not informed of this decision until they received a letter from the company secretary dated 1st November 1962. For some reason, there was a two-month interval between the directors selling, and the members being told of the decision.

An interesting aspect of the site being acquired by the Prudential is that following the tragic fire in 1887, the Prudential was one of the companies that had insured the lives of many victims. Strange that some 75 years later the company was to take over the actual building, although even that did not last, for in 1993 the new building, known now as Portland House, was standing empty and for sale. It later became office accommodation.

Various artefacts from the former Theatre Royal can still be found, including the theatre model once located in the box office, and a fire axe from backstage more recently housed in The Old Fire House, now a public house but formerly a fire station that stood just two buildings away from the Theatre. Mr William Hubbard has the keys and brass handles of the main theatre doors. Six engravings by William Hogarth, entitled "Marriage a la Mode", formerly hanging in the theatre manager's office are said to have been salvaged from the 1887 fire, and were at one time on display in Portland House. However, over the past forty years the building has changed ownership and been redecorated and it would appear that these engravings have now been lost. In the Papermakers Arms, Exe Street, are some of the illuminated signs from the auditorium that former landlord Ken Ellis erected. The circle bar had a splendid chandelier, and that is now in a private residence in the city. There has been frequent suggestion that the large oil paintings, formerly adorning the circle walls, were purchased by the Rougemont Hotel, and hung in their Cavendish room. There is, however, good reason to accept that this is not so and that having been purchased at the auction, the paintings are retained privately in the city.

Thus, in the space of just over 100 years the full circle had been completed. From what had been the gutted remains of a fire-ravished building, Exeter saw another theatre established, only for it to be closed and sold. Upon the same site was witnessed the building of a modern office block – and that, too, was to be sold, having been standing idle for a comparatively short time, before being utilised again. It has always been said that there was a ghost in the Theatre Royal; a page-boy was supposed to haunt the under-stage area, although no evidence of his actual sighting has ever been shown. If ghosts do exist, and if they have any power over man, then perhaps this was some revenge being taken for the Theatre having been closed!

The late George Northcott, a wealthy local benefactor, had tried to save the Theatre from closure. He lived at Nutwell Court, Lympstone, and was a keen supporter of the Arts. Following the news of the impending closure of the Theatre he appointed representatives to enter into discussions with the board of directors with a view to injecting capital. His doctor had advised that he should not enter into any such discussions personally, due to his poor health. He was said to have been ready to use funds from a trust he had set up for the benefit of the county of Devon. According to the directors, his proposals of how the financial assistance he was prepared to put forward should be used were apparently not acceptable. Northcott wanted to involve representatives of the arts, music and drama, and use the Theatre Royal as both a theatre and cultural centre.

Details of the discussions between the board and George Northcott's agents are, of course, not known. However, in May 1962 the *Express & Echo* reported that he was prepared to set up a trust of £100,000, of which about £60,000

138. Portland House, erected in 1963 on the site of the former theatre. The site was purchased by the Prudential Assurance Company, which had been insurers to many victims of the 1887 theatre fire. The brick building on the left stands on the site of the former Blue Star Garage, and there is still an alleyway between the buildings that was formerly called Stable Yard.

would be for the purchase of the actual building. In November of that year, the same source reports that Mr Norman Capener, one of George Northcott's representatives, claimed that whilst the £100,000 for a trust fund was still on offer, not more than £42,000 would be for the purchase of the building. (It is worth noting here that when the Northcott Theatre was agreed upon, his contribution was in fact £100,000) This trust would have saved the theatre from being sold to developers, and the offer was some £15,000 more than the Theatre Royal actually realised at its sale. It appears, however, that the stumbling block was not the total sum, but the figure put on the value of the property itself. Northcott originally suggested £35,000 for the building, with the residue going towards improvements and the creation of an arts and cultural centre. This offer he later increased to £40,000 and a final offer of £42,000.

In short, it seems that the directors convinced the shareholders that it would be preferable to take the £85,000 and close the Theatre, rather than take £42,000 and have a further £58,000 available to preserve the building and maintain a theatre and arts centre in the city. In hindsight it is easy to argue as to whether this was, or was not a sensible move. At the time it was a most controversial and difficult decision to make.

Whilst he did not succeed in preventing the Theatre Royal from being closed, he did maintain his interest in the Arts locally. Following the sale of the Theatre site, George Northcott put up a substantial amount to assist Exeter University in building what was to become the Northcott Theatre, on the University campus. Together with additional financial backing from the Gulbenkian Foundation, this trust was to ensure a Theatre would re-open in Exeter. Sadly, George Northcott did not see his project completed, as he died in 1963.

The Future

In the Editorial column of the *Express & Echo* of 17th September, 1962, the future of the Theatre Royal was discussed under a quotation from Shakespeare's *Julius Caesar* 'There is a tide in the affairs of men when, taken at the flood, leads on to fortune'. The editorial questioned whether it was too late to take that tide. Sadly, it was indeed too late and the Theatre closed a few days later. There was no future for that building, and certainly no fortune.

Our story has been told, but of course it cannot end there. Theatre in some form will always remain with us, as it has done for many centuries. It may not be as we know it today, and perhaps it may not continue in the way many would prefer it to go; but there can be little doubt that show business, dramatic entertainment, theatre – call it what you will – simply has to continue in some form for at least the foreseeable future.

Exeter's 'theatre' has evolved over many years, and will keep doing so because there will always be change and demand. Strolling players were encouraged, and they formed larger groups of entertainers. These larger groups formed companies that played in various buildings and on open ground. Later still, buildings were specifically designed for such dramatic performances. This pattern will surely continue, ensuring future generations some form of theatrical entertainment.

The Theatre Royal was, without doubt, part of this city's heritage for many decades. Its position in the city centre ensured that even those who had no interest in theatre were aware of its existence. It was a part of the city, a part of growing up for many citizens, and even today is talked of with fond memories. That was summed up by an anonymous person, using the pseudonym 'an Exonian in exile', in an article for the *Express & Echo* in November 1959. That person stated that whilst he was away from the city for much of his time, particularly during the two world wars, whenever he returned the highlight of his visit was a few hours at the Theatre Royal. 'To me', he said, 'the old Theatre was Exeter'. He was dismayed when he came home on one occasion and saw that the theatre advertised films! A few years later he was delighted that the 'live theatre' had once more claimed back its audiences. One wonders what the 'Exonian in exile' would think today if he travelled along New North Road towards the city centre?

Many of those who fondly remember the Theatre Royal would welcome a similar theatre in the city today. The former theatre holds many dear memories for many local people, perhaps because they regularly attended the shows there, or maybe because they worked there. Even those who saw only the annual pantomime will recall the many hours they sat enthralled by the antics on stage during those winter nights. There is no doubt that the Theatre Royal meant something to a large number of people.

Progress, of course, means improvement and change in many respects. Why is it, though, that we will abhor the demolition of buildings connected with the arts, rather than, say, a more commercial building such as a bank? Which building has more influence on our lives – the social one or the business one? Over the years Exeter has seen many fine buildings demolished in some way, whether by enemy action, developers or council decisions. Even some existing buildings, erected in this city around the time the Theatre Royal was demolished, are themselves in danger of demolition today, and some have already gone.

Any large public theatre requires a vast amount of financial injection to ensure its survival. The chance for Exeter's council to take over the Theatre Royal was lost, but it has to be said that since the end of the last war other councils have 'taken the plunge' and many theatres are still in existence as a result. Sunderland Council purchased The Empire 'as an investment in the city's future'. Bristol Corporation decided to take over their Theatre Royal when it was threatened with closure, and Cardiff Council did likewise at The New Theatre. The classic example, though, has to be the Gaiety Theatre and Opera House in Douglas, Isle of Man. In 1971 the Isle of Man government purchased a rather sadly neglected building with the intention of saving it for posterity. Today, just over one hundred years since it was built, it is a sight to behold, having been painstakingly restored to its former glory. It is virtually impossible to describe in words just what has been achieved there. This may be a unique jewel in the crown of theatre refurbishment, but it proves that it is far from impossible to save theatres from extinction.

So what of the future for theatre in Exeter? We have no former theatre to restore, and although many people would welcome 'another Theatre Royal' in the city centre, it is only too obvious that although that may be desirable, there are now very few suitable locations. The current proposals for developing the city's central area do not include any proposals for a new theatre or concert hall. We are often reminded that we already have the Northcott and Barnfield Theatres, both of which continue to serve Exeter's theatre going public. Yet neither is capable of an audience capacity anywhere near that of the former Theatre Royal, which was able to accommodate over 900 people. In recent years it has been pointed out in the press on numerous occasions that anyone in Exeter wanting to see larger, and perhaps more spectacular, shows, has to travel to Plymouth or Bristol, and it is not difficult to understand why that is the case. Should they really have to go elsewhere? Should this city be able provide for them?

Tastes change, of course, and the tastes of today's public differs considerably from the days of the Theatre Royal, with a far greater choice of theatrical and other entertainment. The millions of pounds required to produce some of the lavish spectacles of today's theatre contrasts starkly with the comparatively meagre budgets on which the Theatre Royal tried to exist. Yet any show requires not only cash, but also audiences, and without them no show can be contemplated. Surely Devon's capital city should have a suitable venue for large shows, concerts and the like, where audiences could be attracted rather than allowed to go elsewhere. It would require a suitably central location, a vast financial outlay, and need considerable sponsorship to maintain; but it has been proved by others that it is not an impossible task.

Theatre is a world of fantasy and make-believe; perhaps it is fantasy to expect the future to produce anything on the lines of the Theatre Royal; perhaps it is make-believe to suggest that a new theatre can be any more successful than those we already have in the city. Whilst it is easy to remember the good times, it is perhaps more difficult to understand the empty seats and lack of income. Many in Exeter and the surrounding areas still lament the passing of the Theatre Royal. Their dream is of a replacement that would bring back to this city that certain something which *was* 'theatre'. Harry Hopkins, the last Theatre Royal chief electrician, sums up that 'certain something' most vividly:

> The professionalism people talk of when referring to theatre work is what I like to feel to be showmanship. It was a feeling of being responsible for an element in the entertainment and enjoyment of many people at a given time. There was a great feeling of the 'live' show. When I cued the orchestra and my hand started to move the house lights dimmer handle, I could really feel the antici-pation in the audience. The same feeling that I had as a child, waiting for the start of a pantomime.

That, surely, is theatre. If there is any glimmer of hope that dreams can be a reality, then perhaps one day there will be a sign lighting up Exeter's evening skyline, a sign saying "Theatre Royal, Exeter".

Oh! no it won't.

But perhaps, hopefully, oh! yes it will!

CHRISTMAS PANTOMIMES

1889	Jack & The Beanstalk		1926	Jack & The Beanstalk
1890	Aladdin		1927	Aladdin
1891	Dick Whittington		1928	Cinderella
1892	Babes in The Wood		1929	Babes in The Wood
1893	Little Red Riding Hood		1930	Dick Whittington
1894	Ali Baba & The Forty Thieves		1931	Goody Two Shoes
1895	Dick Whittington		1932	Mother Goose
1896	Robinson Crusoe		1933	Sinbad
1897	Bluebeard		1934	Babes in The Wood
1898	Aladdin		1935	Dick Whittington
1899	Cinderella		1936	Cinderella
1900	Puss in Boots		1937	Mother Hubbard
1901	Babes in The Wood		1938	Mother Goose
1902	Sinbad The Sailor		1939	Aladdin
1903	Sleeping Beauty		1940	Jack & The Beanstalk
1904	Robinson Crusoe		1941	Dick Whittington
1905	Jack & The Beanstalk		1942	Aladdin
1906	Aladdin		1943	Cinderella
1907	Dick Whittington		1944	Jack & The Beanstalk
1908	Cinderella		1945	Babes in The Wood
1909	Red Riding Hood		1946	Dick Whittington
1910	Dick Whittington		1947	Cinderella
1911	Aladdin		1948	Mother Goose
1912	Goody Two Shoes		1949	Robinson Crusoe
1913	Robinson Crusoe		1950	Jack & The Beanstalk
1914	Mother Goose		1951	Babes in The Wood
1915	Babes in The Wood		1952	Aladdin
1916	Cinderella		1953	Dick Whittington
1917	Aladdin		1954	Cinderella
1918	Jack & Hill		1955	Jack & The Beanstalk
1919	Aladdin		1956	Mother Goose
1920	Ali Baba		1957	Robinson Crusoe
1921	Sinbad		1958	Cinderella
1922	Cinderella		1959	Dick Whittington
1923	Babes in The Wood		1960	Babes in The Wood
1924	Dick Whittington		1961	Ali Baba
1925	Humpty Dumpty		1962	Theatre closed

BIBLIOGRAPHY

Books

Edwin Adeler and Con West   *Remember Fred Karno?* (John Long, London, 1939)

Eric Delderfield   *Cavalcade by Candlelight* (Delderfield Press, Exmouth, 1950)

Margaret Toms   *The Seventh Star* (Exeter, 1967)

William Cotton   *The Story of the Drama in Exeter* (Hamilton Adams, London, 1887)

Harvey Crane   *Playbill* (MacDonald & Evans, Plymouth, 1980)

Newspapers

Devon & Exeter Gazette

Devon Weekly Times

The Express & Echo

The Graphic

The Illustrated London News

The Pall Mall Gazette

The Penny Illustrated

Trewmans Exeter Flying Post

Western Daily Mercury

The Western Morning News

SUBSCRIBERS

Miss Lisa Abbott
Christine Anning
Prof. P. P. Anthony
Jan Baker
Peter and Mo Barr
Mr Jeffrey Bassett
Mrs Margaret Batten
Miss Diana Beasley
John and Sally Bennett
Mr Peter Bennett
Mrs Joan Bowditch
Mrs Doreen Brailsford
Mr John L. Brewer
John Brooke
Miss M. L. Brown
Mr K. J. Burrow
Mrs Marlene Butler
Ms C. Caldwell
Mrs Christine Caldwell
Mrs Dawn Canham
Ms Marion Carter
Mr Barry Casley
Mrs Joyce Chambers
Miss Anthea Chapman
Mr and Mrs Gordon Chapman
Mr William Chapple
Melvin Conder
Mr and Mrs George Cooke
Roy and Sheila Coombs
Patricia A. Cousins
Robert Crawley
Mr John Cross
Mr Rudolf Miles Crossley
Mrs Edythe Crump
Professor Brian Currah
Mr Dennis Darke
K. J. Davis
Mr Terry Davis
Lady Violet De Vere
Mr Nick Discombe
Mrs Wendy Dyer
Bill and Sue Edmund
Mike Edmund
Nick Edmund
Mr Ray Ellis
Mr Roger Evans
Mr William R. Flack
Maurice and Glenys Fradley

Mr and Mrs Ray Fradley
Dr Paul Fryer
Mrs Heather Galley
Mrs Margaret Gay
Mrs B. J. Gibbs
Russ and Marion Gill
M. R. Gordon-Wright
Mrs Jean Green
Dr and Mrs Peter Gurney
Mrs Ann Hayman
Mr and Mrs Alan Hine
Mr Don Hodge
Peter and Susan Holwell
Mrs Ruth House
Mrs F. W. Howard
Mr and Mrs William Dudley
    Hubbard
Mrs Vi Hurn
Don and Mary Hutchings
Mrs Heather Hutton
Ted Hynds and Mrs Reagan
Mrs Sue Jackson
Mr William Jackson
Mrs Julie Jeary
Mrs E. Myra Jones
Mr R. C. Kenyon
Mrs Betty Kerslake
Mrs Joy King
Miss Meneen Kingsford-
    Lethbridge
Mrs Rae Knight
Mrs Margaret Knowles
Mr Robert Knowling
Mr John Langabeer
Mr Brian Le Messurier
Mr C. R. Laskey
Mr Ed Lee
Miss Marjorie Leeds
Mr Michael Littley
Dr Leon H. Long
Mr Michael C. Long
Mr Colin Mapledoram
Mr David Marston
Graham and Jennie Martin
Viv Martyn
Mr Anthony John May
Miss Elizabeth Maycock
Mrs Irene Mogridge

Chris Morgan
Trevor Morson
Mr and Mrs Ian Newman
Mr and Mrs John Parkin
Graham and Jan Parnell
Mike and Jane Passmore
Mona Passmore
Mr Mark Pattenden
Mrs Frances Peers
Mr Eric A. Pickard
Mrs Joy Pitts
Mrs Pat Pollard
Mr Frank Potter
Mr George Pridmore
Mrs Patricia Purchese
Mr Richard Purton
Michael and Gina Redman
Mr Chris Robinson
Mr Roderick Ross
C. T. Shears
Mrs Mary D. N. Smith
Mr Keith Spencer
Margaret and Frank Stanbury
Stella Stevenson
Diana and Rick Stewart
Mr J. F. Stirling
Pauline Stringer
Mr and Mrs J. R. B. Sutton
J. V. Swain
Mr Michael Tamlyn
Mr Peter Thomas
Mr and Mrs Jack Tree
Mrs Christine Trigger
Mr Adrian Uzzell
Mrs Marion Vanstone
Mr John Vicary
Mrs Jean Wall
Mr Mike Walker
Susan and Tim Walker
Joy and Derek Warner
Mrs Pearl Webb
Mrs C. M. West
Mrs June Wheatley
Mr Nicholas White
Mrs Doreen E. Whitelock
Mr John Willey
Mrs Joan G. Williams-Hawkes
Mr John R. A. Wilson